Adirondack Fishing in the 1930s

A YORK STATE BOOK

Buttermilk Falls, on the Raquette River between Forked and Long Lakes. Bass were present in the basin at the foot of the falls, but trout could be found in nearby spring holes all through the summer. *Photo by Edward Bierstadt. Adirondack Museum, Blue Mountain Lake, New York.*

Adirondack Fishing in the 1930s

A Lost Paradise

VINCENT ENGELS

SYRACUSE UNIVERSITY PRESS

Copyright © 1978 by SYRACUSE UNIVERSITY PRESS
Syracuse, New York 13244-5160

First Paperback Edition 1994
94 95 96 97 98 99   6 5 4 3 2 1

This book is published with the assistance of a grant from the John Ben Snow Foundation.

Library of Congress Cataloging in Publication Data
Engels, Vincent.
  Adirondack fishing in the 1930s.
  (A York State book)
  1. Fishing—New York (State)—Adirondack Mountains.
I. Title.
SH529.E53   799.1′1′0974753   78-7608
ISBN 0-8156-0291-X

Manufactured in the United States of America

For Bop and Mima
—and all who helped to make this book

VINCENT ENGELS (d. 1992), formerly a newspaperman and for twenty years Editor and Head of Publications Branch, Office of Naval Intelligence, had fished trout, bass, and salmon from Oregon to Nova Scotia and from Georgia to Quebec.

Acknowledgments

I AM PARTICULARLY indebted to Martin H. Pfeiffer, Associate Aquatic Biologist of the State of New York, for voluminous correspondence in recent years on the present condition of the Adirondack fisheries and for letting me have a copy of the historical chapter and other pertinent sections of his encyclopedic in-house document, "A Proposed Fisheries Management Proposal for the Adirondacks"; to Charles L. Todd, Professor Emeritus of Hamilton College and member of the Adirondack League Club, for his powerful and vivid commentary in the Afterword on the present condition of Adirondack waters; to William K. Verner, Curator of the Adirondack Museum, for reading the manuscript and noting a number of points to be modified or checked for accuracy, and for providing scenic photographs from the files of the Museum; to Robert F. Hall, retired Editor, and John H. DuPont, Editor of *The Conservationist,* for encouragement to proceed with these recollections of fishing and fishermen of the 1930s; to Edward Wallace of Long Lake, Edward H. Griffin of Blue Mountain, Donald M. Moodie of East Hamilton, N.J., Charles E. Boone and James F. Lord of New York State's Forest Protection and

Fire Management Division, for checking and refreshing my memories of men and events, and to Robert W. Rehbaum, Chief, Bureau of Audio-Visual Services of the Department of Environmental Conservation, Alice Emery Cyr, W. L. Engels, Lynn McCane, Sarah Marran Noble, George Smith, Jr., and Martin Pfeiffer for photographs.

Annapolis, Maryland   Vincent Engels
Spring 1978

Contents

Adirondack Fishing in the 1930s

The Scene

THE YEAR IS 1936. From the top of Mount Kempshall, midway along the east shore of Long Lake, Mr. Jesse Russell the fire observer looks southwest to Mr. Harry Bowker's station in the tower on Owl's Head, and slightly west of due south to where Mr. Bert Wells is observing the scene from the tower on Blue Mountain. They have most of the central Adirondacks around and between them. What is blocked from Mr. Bowker's view by a rise of ground, as Buck Mountain cuts off sight of Follansby Pond, is laid out like a map for Mr. Russell and vice versa. Mr. Wells overlaps some territory of the others but has his own view of lands east and south that they cannot see.

The smoke up Cold River valley in the northeast that Mr. Bowker cannot see is visible to Mr. Russell but gives him no concern. It comes from the camp fire of Mr. Noah J. Rondeau, on the bank of the river above an old logging dam. Mr. Rondeau is a hermit. In another fifteen years or so books and articles will be written about him and he will become a petted figure at the annual Sportsmen's

1

Shows in New York City. Now he is known only to the few hikers and anglers who pass by, to the game protectors of Tupper Lake, and of course to Mr. Russell. This morning he sits quietly in the cabin yard reading *The Western Christian Messenger*. The air is quiet and muggy here this morning, and he is smudging against the black flies, so the smoke that Mr. Russell sees is denser than usual. The life of Mr. Rondeau, the hermit, living off his potato patch and the game he can kill, secure in his domain behind his signs warning off the guardians of the law, reading a little basic astronomy for his pleasure and devotional literature for flaws to document his opinion of the preachers, is a favorite topic of Mr. Russell's.

Mr. Russell has the best possible view of the Seward Mountains, their summit eleven miles away, of the peaks of Santanoni, southeast of Seward, and of the valley of Cold River between them. Boiling Pond, where the trout grow long and lean on a diet of leeches, lies in one of the folds of Seward. So does the Lost Pond that Mr. Abbott and Bige Smith found after its location had been lost for a generation, and, in this year of 1936, after another lapse of thirty years, has not been revisited.

Mr. Russell also has the best view of Long Lake and of the lower Raquette River, turning abruptly westward for several miles where it meets the flanks of Seward, then resuming its northerly course to gather in the flow of the Moose Ponds and Follansby, where Emerson and his cronies camped in the summer of 1858: "Ten men, ten guides, our company all told . . ."

> Northward the length of Follansbee we rowed,
> Under low mountains, whose unbroken ridge
> Ponderous with beechen forest sloped the shore.

2

Mr. Russell's mountain sits astride a watershed. East and south he overlooks waters that flow to the Hudson River. Long Lake on the west and its Cold River tributary to the north go down the Raquette to the St. Lawrence.

The woods on Kempshall are full of deer. The visitor notes that the plants in Mr. Russell's garden at the foot of the tower are all growing under wire cages—all except the potato plants. Deer do not care for potato vines, but they eat anything else the gardener grows. They come to the tower every night, paw around in the soft earth, and snort indignantly when they find the wire cages and smell the human beings asleep in the cabin nearby.

Mr. Russell, Mr. Wells, and Mr. Bowker are often on the phone to each other. It is not always a matter of smoke in the valleys. When we visited Mr. Russell earlier today he was in conversation with Mr. Bowker on Owl's Head. Some visitor to the Owl's Head tower, preparing to descend, had just bumped into Mr. Bowker's shepherd puppy and knocked her through the open hatch. A hind leg caught on a beam, and Mr. Bowker was able to grab it and haul her back. He said to Mr. Russell that the park authorities should not allow casual visitors to climb the tower. Mr. Russell agreed, out of sympathy for the dog, but said, out of courtesy to us, that the visitors did help to pass the time.

Of the three fire lookouts, Mr. Wells on Blue Mountain has by far the most visitors. Through July and August not a half hour passes that does not bring a new batch to the summit. Blue Mountain is more accessible than Owl's Head or Kempshall, and it has the more spectacular water views. Blue Mountain Lake, the Marion River, and Raquette Lake are spread out below to the southwest, and at higher levels many little alpine ponds are scattered like rain pools in the hollows of the mountains.

3

Blue Mountain from Raquette Lake Village. *New York State Department of Environmental Conservation.*

Very close to the face of the mountain in the northeast, and eighteen hundred feet below the tower, lies Tirrell Pond, its water clear as air, and its beaches perhaps the whitest in the park. The name comes from one of four young Vermont families that set out in the summer of 1830 without guides, maps, or any clear idea of where they would wind up, to find new homes for themselves. Their story, based on local lore, has been told by Henry Abbott. A few weeks of trekking up hill and down through the dense forest, their way west blocked by the rivers and lakes of the central Adirondacks, they became disheartened and settled on the

4

Salmon River, an inlet of South Pond between Blue Mountain and Long Lake. Toward spring of the following year all died of a plague but the ten-year-old son of the Tirrells who was found wandering in the woods and given a home by an Indian trapper. Ten or more years later this one survivor of "the plague settlement" built his own home on the shores of the pond that has been named for him.

Across the deep valley in which is Tirrell Pond rises Dun Brook Mountain. Its summit is less than four airline miles from Mr. Wells's tower. It was in that valley and on the flanks of Dun Brook Mountain that a stranger who lived as a hermit, much in the manner of Mr. Rondeau on Cold River, was hunted down and killed by state troopers and the men of Blue Mountain in the winter of 1932. Mr. Wells found it a disturbing story, reflected on it endlessly, and had much to say of it to his visitors and to his friend Mr. Bowker on occasion.

To visit Mr. Bowker on Owl's Head you must first go up Long Lake by canoe or guideboat from Deerland to the mouth of Owl's Head Brook. You can climb to the tower in an hour by moving right along or, taking it easy, an hour and a half. At the top the whole country opens up. To right, left, and all about are the mountains—long, angular ridges, round tops, and pointed peaks—and between them the lakes are spread, their colors varying with the cloud shadows and the distance.

Southwest Mr. Bowker overlooks some of the bays and arms of Forked Lake and one of its islands. The main body of the lake is hidden, but he points out the western arm where Brandreth Stream winds down to it through marshland. The squaretails of Forked move into Brandreth Stream late in the summer. We shall be fishing there on quiet evenings and overcast days in August.

5

The smoke on the south shore of Forked, Mr. Bowker says, is from Bob Glasbrook's place. We know Bob as a gardener and boatman. He sells us minnows, rents us a boat when we do not have one with us, and allows us to put up the tent on his shore. We lunch in his kitchen on roast spring chicken from his hen house, vegetables fresh from the garden within the hour, and a bottle of his excellent home brew, all for one dollar. Bob is a large, fat man, but Mr. Bowker tells us that he is "quicker than a cat and a great fighter. He cleared out a bar in Tupper Saturday night. You heard? Four men ganged up on him. No reason except he refused to drink with them. Bob's face looks like he's been in a wreck, but two of the men are in the hospital. I know he seems a mild, quiet man, and that he is. But don't get rough with Bob. All he asks is a little respect, what a man's entitled to."

To the west of Owl's Head, as far south as Forked Lake, and from there to the northwest and north for many miles, Mr. Bowker overlooks the expansive acres of the Whitney estate and some of the most productive squaretail waters in the east—Charley Pond Stream, Little Tupper Lake, Grampus and Mohegan Lakes, Bog Stream, and Handsome Pond among them. No one knows their spring holes better than Duke Austin, the garage owner of Long Lake Village, known as the Duke because he is one of those men born to lead, to inspire others, to fish, to dance, to amuse, to do everything in a manner and style above the reach of common men. Poaching as ordinarily practiced is altogether too shoddy, furtive, and demeaning for such a man. To give the game some stature, and in the name of fair play, he graciously calls up Superintendent Potter to inform him that it is his intention to fish Charley Pond or Bog Stream sometime during the night. He was apprehended at it once, summoned to court, and fined $25 for the trespass. "Worth every penny," said the Duke. "They have to win one sometime or there'd be no fun in it," with a laugh that made everybody happy.

Due east Mr. Bowker sees the timbered wall of East Inlet Mountain and behind it the long, sweeping outlines of Fishing Brook Mountain and its nearby peaks, palely colored and seeming to stand farther away than they are because of the soft haze that surrounds them.

At the foot of East Inlet Mountain is the village of Deerland. At Deerland the old-time Adirondack accents can still be heard, unchanged from the time of the first Plumleys and Austins, although absent from the speech of Saranac and Old Forge years ago. Deerland is the site of a lodge where people stay who want to get away from the city summer. A noted inventor, woodsman, and angler, Mr. Henry Abbott, is among them.

Deerland is also the home of Bige Smith, his brother-in-law Sam Smith, and their families. Bige, who arrived at Deerland in 1888, has been employed since 1890 as a guide by Mr. Abbott. Mr. Abbott's stories of the woods almost invariably begin with "Bige and I. . . ." Following his lead, Bige begins with "I and Abbott. . . ." Bige's brother-in-law Sam keeps the vegetable gardens for the Deerland Lodge and in winter repairs and re-varnishes the classic guideboats built by Bige's brother George Smith, now passed away. Sam has George's patterns in the loft of the boat shop and can be coaxed into building a boat himself, but it takes some doing and you must be prepared to wait a year or two before he gets around to it.

To the southeast of Mr. Bowker's lookout is an immense gulf. The visitor is on the rim of the domed rock which gives the mountain its name. The rock drops straight

7

View of lower Long Lake, with the Seward Mountains in the background. Once exclusively a trout lake, it has been taken over by smallmouth bass, pike, and yellow perch. *Photo by S. R. Stoddard. Adirondack Museum, Blue Mountain Lake, New York.*

away below; its cracks and clefts support flowers, herbs, small firs, and one rowan tree, a hundred feet down, that holds its berries above the gulf.

The lowland, heavily wooded, pitches toward the upper end of Long Lake. Beyond the lake, the forest opens up again to disclose South Pond and then begins an uninterrupted march to Blue Mountain, riding the air like a ship.

People have been climbing Owl's Head to see the landscape since the first settlers came to Long Lake around 1830. In 1846 some native volunteered to guide Mr. J. T. Headley and his party to the top. Mr. Headley was a preacher who had come to the wilderness for the sake of his constitution, which was in need of fresh air and exercise. There was no trail up the mountain in those days. The guide lost his way, and the party was nine hours getting to the top. They had brought no food with them, since they had expected to be gone only half that time, and Mr. Headley became so famished that he offered one of his friends five dollars for a cigar "to stimulate my exhausted system." A doctor in the party ate some venison that he had been carrying in his pocket for use as trout bait—"A Frenchman could not have wished it older," wrote Mr. Headley—and they all ate the leaves of sheep's sorrel on the way down. They lost the way again and were five hours more getting back to the settlement, where Mr. Headley threw himself on the floor "and begged most piteously for a morsel of food."

Mr. Headley did not like the mountain's name, Owl's Head, since it had nothing to justify it but its shape. "A forester here has requested me to give it a name, promising it shall keep it." Fortunately the promise was not kept, or we would have still another mountain burdened like Marcy, Colden, and so many others with the name of a forgotten worthy in a land where all the names should be Indian names, which are descriptive, or translations thereof.

No place on earth has held me in such a spell as the Adirondacks in the 1930s.

9

I was born and raised in northeastern Wisconsin, a green and fertile country of many rivers under a high, broad sky. A walk of two or three miles took me to the woods and hills on our side of town. A street car ride to the other side, followed by a two-mile walk, brought me to a trout stream.

My college years were spent in northern Indiana, a land of small, clear, spring-fed lakes, fragrant marshes, dunes that were then untrammelled, and nearby the great blue lake of Michigan.

There was a year in the city of Paris, then at its most glamorous and hospitable to the stranger, especially if he were young and not well funded.

Later there was Maryland with its Chesapeake Bay, to the westward rolling hills, and still farther west the limestone spurs and crags of the Blue Ridge, in season clad with masses of flowering dogwood and laurel.

I was happy to be in all these places, but what I felt for the Adirondacks was a fulfillment beyond happiness. I had seen them first, five or six years before I could have guessed that I might spend some summers there, hitchhiking down from Canada with a college friend on the road that hugs the west shore of Lake Champlain. It was a drizzly day in early June, not many cars on the road, and we hiked more miles than we hitched. That was all right with me. The dark and piled-up land with the rain cloud covering its summits, so darkly and ponderously beautiful, had me enthralled. I had a strong sense of *déjà vu*. Had I believed in a previous existence, I would have thought that I was returning to a land where I had once lived and been torn from much against my will.

In later years I remember the excitement in the car as somewhere around Saratoga we caught the first glimpse

This two-day catch was made by James A. Emery and Clint Sutton on Grassy Pond, between Cranberry Lake and Bog River. The pond, like so many other Adirondack waters, no longer holds trout.

of the mountains in the distance, and an hour later the surge of elation as we rounded a bend and Blue Mountain filled the sky before us.

Soon we would be back in the great forest, its trails blanketed in pine needles, its back country ponds and rivers undisturbed as yet by the outboard motor, the angler's only rivals the otter and the heron. The scene, the setting, was the great attraction, but the fishing had its own importance. Nowhere but in the Canadian wild or the more remote waters of Maine could you have found such squaretail trout, heavy bodied, with jewelled sides, dark green-blue vermiculated backs, and underbellies that as August nights began to cool were transformed from dusky pearl to flaming purplish red. It was the true native strain, adulterated through stocking in later years. Elsewhere a brook trout of one pound honest weight was a season's trophy, but here fish of twice that size, although not to be had near the highways, were not uncommon off the beaten track, and four- to five-pounders could still be found. Elsewhere the daylight fly fishing was over by the third week of June, but here in the high-altitude waters it went on throughout the summer. There was not as much of it left as in the camping days of Henry Abbott—when there had already been some falloff from the heyday of Reuben Wood—but what remained in the spring holes of the Raquette and the Cedar, in those of great Cranberry and its inlets, in Grassy Pond and Handsome, in the ponds on Seward, and at the foot of Marcy was probably as good as ever, although it was not to remain much longer so.

Long Lake and the Raquette River

AT THE FOOT of Owl's Head Mountain the Raquette River spills into a valley that is fourteen miles long southwest to northeast, barely half a mile wide in places, double that at the widest. The valley is guarded by the Owl's Head and Buck Mountains on the west, by East Inlet, Sabattis, Blueberry, and Kempshall on the east. Across the end of the valley rises the massif of the Seward Range.

The river is the principal feeder of Long Lake but not the only one. Coming in from the west as we proceed down the lake shore are the outlet streams of Owl's Head Pond, Lake Eaton (known as Clear Pond in the early thirties), Grampus Lake, Rock Pond, and the three Anthony Ponds. From the east come the waters of South Pond and its tributary ponds, Salmon and Mud.

With its wooded islands, its granite ledges sliding to the water, its fragrant marshes where the ledges give way, it is a very beautiful lake, and the visitor is not surprised to learn that at one time, little more than a century ago, it was exclusively trout water, known for the size and abundance of its squaretails.* In 1880, when Mr. Henry Abbott first came to the lake, trout were still the predominant fish; ten years later a fateful thinning of their numbers was only too apparent. There were still some trout to be found off its spring brooks in the first years of the twentieth century, however. "Used to be I and Abbott could go down to that cove on the other side of Pine Point, whar the cold spring comes in, and get trout for supper any time at all," said Bige Smith in 1931. "But not since some time before the war."

By the time I first fished there, in 1931, only the tributary waters—and not all of those—still had trout. It was rumored that a few large squaretails were still hiding out in Mud Pond and Upper Sargent and could be caught after heavy rains when the brooks were coming down in freshets. We tried for them many times but saw no evidence of trout and naturally came to question how reliable and recent this intelligence might be. The Sargent Ponds had splendid fishing for small mouth bass, however, and in Mud Pond every cast of any fly was taken by a bass of six to eight inches in length while three others of his class rushed to grab it from him. A bass nursery it was, but not a trout pond.

Long Lake too had its bass, and these were large

* Genio C. Scott, publishing in 1875, made note also of a "Red Trout of Long Lake," describing it as "the richest and most beautiful specimen of lake trout known in the State of New York . . . reddish-brown on the back, mellowing to a pink at the sides, and a belly of white with a pink tinge. The whole of its surface, except its head and belly, is thickly dotted with orange specks the size of pigeon-shot." I have met such fishes in my dreams, although not recently. Mr. Martin Pfeiffer informs me that a lake trout of ordinary coloration was among the fish netted during a study of Long Lake in 1966—an escapee from Lake Eaton or a remnant population, who knows?

14

ones. It also had whitefish—not many, but large. The bass were common, especially off the rocky shoals and ledges. The whitefish were few and confined to the deep holes near the lower end of the lake. Only a few guides knew about them and kept the secret close. The bass had been introduced by the state fish authorities in 1872; whether the whitefish were native or not I have been unable to determine.

The trout of Long Lake had long been gone by the year 1931, but pike abounded. They had been brought to Long Lake by a pair of native citizens—Rob Shaw and Lysander Hall—for reasons known only to themselves, some time before 1880.

Mr. Abbott, who had been fishing Long Lake since 1880, and Bige Smith, who had arrived at Deerland in 1888, said it was the pike that had made off with the trout, and they were probably right. Other than the presence of pike and bass, the lake itself had not changed much since the 1890s. Deerland and Long Lake village were still tiny hamlets, and there were miles of shoreline without a camp in sight. Why the pike had not yet cleaned out the whitefish was a mystery, however. Bass and trout coexist peacefully in Raquette River, Cedar River, and elsewhere, but pike and trout are another story.

The village of Long Lake once decided to create a trout pond out of the marsh in the heart of town. Through this marsh Shaw Brook ran in several channels. Above the town, Shaw Brook was a good little trout stream, so there was no question about the quality of its water. A dam was built across the mouth of the brook; the channel and marsh were then treated with rotenone to get rid of the trash fish, and the pond was allowed to fill. Several thousand trout of the six-inch class were stocked and the pond closed to all

15

James A. Emery heading up Long Lake toward Raquette River inlet.

fishing for two full years to give them a chance to grow. For a time they did well. At evening that first summer, the townsmen would gather to watch the fish rising all over the pond to gnats and midges. On one of those evenings Mr. Duke Austin, whose own feats of poaching have passed into legend, let it be known that any one so far down the ladder of manliness as to snitch a trout from the town's own pond had best start off at the same time for parts unknown. So there were no violations of sanctuary, yet when spring arrived, there seemed to be fewer fish. By the end of that second summer there were none at all to be seen, whereupon

16

a net was stretched across the sluice and the dam opened. No trout were found in the net, but it did hold some fat pike that had survived the rotenone and been foraging at will in this paradise of a trout pond where angling was not permitted. One of them weighed sixteen pounds.

Pike of more than twenty pounds and smallmouth bass of more than four were caught every year in Long Lake. I never got any of these overgrown fish myself, although I came close several times. Once a huge pike grabbed the plug within a few feet of the boat and threw water all over me. I reacted by clamping both thumbs to the reel; the plug popped to the surface with a hook broken off and holes punched through the baked enamel. The fish was hurt and leaped three or four times along the edge of the weed beds, coming clear of the water and twisting violently. To this day I feel unhappy about that wounded fish, trying so frantically to shake the iron from its jaw. Next morning a pike described as enormous floated ashore on a neighbor's beach, but I did not hear about it until a week later, by which time it had been buried in the neighbor's flower garden, with some ceremony too, I understand, the neighbor being a clerical man.

One of the best places for bass was the rocky basin where the Raquette River tumbles into Long Lake. We rowed slowly up and down here, casting bass bugs and streamers to the rocks and snags, and then anchored near a large rock in the middle and drifted live minnows. I had a fat lively chub on the rig one day that was strong enough to pull the bobber under water and keep it there for several seconds of suspense. Finally the bobber disappeared with a chug and the line moved swiftly down current. This was something else again. I let it run, waiting for the usual pause and the start of a second run before striking, but

17

there was no pause. More line flew out and with only a few turns left on the reel, the fish turned on full speed and was streaking for the lake. I reared back on the rod—a good stout Shakespeare fly rod with double spiral wrappings—and broke it in two at the lower ferrule. At this, all pull left the line as though the fish had dropped the bait. I reeled in and found the line cut cleanly through. This fish must have been another large pike, for of course a bass could not have cut the line. A visiting lady who was in the boat with us, seeing me rather pensive on the way back, thought to cheer me by saying I should not feel badly about the rod, as such an accident could happen to anyone. But it was not of the rod I was thinking, much as I had prized it, but of the fish that had had the weight and power to break it in the butt. There was a seven-inch snell of treble-twisted gut attached to the hook, too. The chub must have been held far back in the jaws for the teeth to have chopped through the line above the snell.

Another time I was casting from the bow of the canoe when Ed Wallace, who was dragging a plug behind the stern, hooked what he thought was a bundle of weed. I heard the reel click slowly and Ed say, "Damn, I did not know there was any weed back there," and I turned around in time to see a large swirling boil on the surface.

"You have a good pike there, Ed," I said, whereupon the grandest of smallmouth bass cleared the surface in a graceful arching leap and the plug dropped free. Bass of four to five pounds had been brought to camp occasionally, but this specimen was of another class entirely.

Next morning I rolled out of bed at five o'clock to get a crack at him, but a voice from the window said: "Go back to bed. Ed is out there already in the canoe." Not that it did him any good. Two weeks later a young girl caught

18

our noble leaper on a minnow. It weighed just one ounce under eight pounds and was a *Field and Stream* prize winner that year for the northern division.

Long Lake, since we lived beside it, was reserved for an occasional Sunday afternoon when time and the family dinner hour did not permit a trip elsewhere. When we wanted a full day's bass fishing, we took the guide boat to one of the outlying ponds—Sargent's or Slim or to Forked Lake. The ponds had the most consistent fishing; action was always lively at either one. Forked could be dull or very exciting—you never knew what you might strike in the way of bass, trout, or salmon. We felt drawn to Forked, even after repeated disappointments, because of these occasional successes and its wild beauty. The southern shore was nearly all state forest, the northern was part of the Whitney family's 100,000 acres. One Whitney camp was located on an arm of the lake, and that was the only structure of any kind along the shoreline except for a state lean-to. Brandreth Stream came down to it through a lovely open marsh, and the Raquette River through a lane in the tall hardwoods. One could take a boat up either of these inlets with great expectations—of bass in the Raquette or trout in Brandreth—but come back with just the opposite. A day on Forked—with its densely wooded shoreline, its bays and capes retreating and advancing, the balanced contrast of light and shade, as if laid out by a painter of the Hudson River school—was an elegant experience whether we had luck or not. The water was so clear and good we drank it freely. The thin-bladed oar of the guide-boat dipped into it with a crisp, crackling sound, leaving a

19

swirl with a vortex that would last until the boat had passed four strokes beyond, and meanwhile seem to have been carved into the surface of the lake.

The deep spring holes in Forked held large, deep-bellied squaretails that as summer waned moved up into Brandreth Stream. Forked also had some landlocked salmon. From time to time, when the surface was not ruffled by wind, you would see one break over the deep in the middle of the lake. In our first years we spent some hours chasing these breaks with a fly rod at the ready. By the time we got there the fish were always elsewhere and we would be casting over empty water. One day as we parked at the landing, two men were just pulling up in their boat. When we asked what luck, they said they had caught two large rainbows. "But it's funny, they don't have any color in this lake." What they held up was a pair of three-pound landlocks.

Raquette River itself in the last century had a large stock of native trout. I have seen no record to indicate how far downriver the trout ranged. Chittenden in 1864 caught four pounders at the mouth of Cold River and probably they could have been found where other good streams come in all the way to the St. Lawrence. By the 1930s, however, they were not in the river below Long Lake. Above the lake, both in the stretch to Forked and still higher up between Forked and Raquette, there were trout in the spring holes of the river throughout the summer. The rocky basin at the foot of Buttermilk Falls looked like classic trout water, but here through July and August we caught only small bass. Sixty feet downriver was a pocket of quiet water along the far bank that looked like a hangout for bass. This was the trout hole. A tiny trickle of cold water coming down to the river through the moss and rocks made it so.

In the middle of the rapids below Raquette Lake at low water time. Trout were found here earlier in the season, smallmouth bass in August.

You had to wade the heavy rapids and cross the river to fish it properly, but the effort was worth it.

Somewhat farther downriver the rapids flattened out into a deep, long, eddying pool, and in this pool we might catch trout or bass. The middle reaches of the pool had to be fished from a canoe, but the upper end could be covered well enough by wading. We were there one morning when three fish were swirling sedately and at regular intervals like large trout feeding just beneath the surface. My small black nymph was taken with a hard tug, and as there were no acrobatics I was confident I had a big squaretail on the hook. It turned out to be a two-pound bass. The second fish took the fly and fought in the same way. Another bass. The third broke off soon after being hooked, so we could not tell what it was or what it might have done. Each of the two fish I netted had the little nymph deep in its throat, which may have had something to do with their not taking to the air.

The best trout I saw taken from this pool was one of eighteen inches and two and a half pounds, caught by my father-in-law, Mr. James A. Emery (Bop). From time to time we heard of bigger fish there. Mr. Biekbehn, a state conservation official we sometimes fished with, reported getting a three-pounder. At daybreak on another morning Mr. Emery was working along the far side of the pool, trying to get at the seldom-fished middle reaches. The brush was dense here and there was deep water close to the bank. He stepped out on a log to position himself for a roll cast, and as he did a very large trout came out from beneath him and swam slowly toward the deeps. This fish, which he had ample opportunity to see clearly in all its length and noble girth, he judged could not have been less than six to seven pounds.

From the big pool downriver to the lake were just two pockets of water that held trout in summer, each one marked by a trickle of water coming down the bank. There we could usually count on taking several fish of the eight-to ten-inch class. You had to stay well hidden, of course, and let the leader fall across large boulders so that its shadow would not alarm the trout in the clear shallow water. Only the fly and a bit of the leader point touched the water. You could not see what was going on but struck at the sound of the rise. Here one morning I was surprised by a tug that broke the leader. Next day I came back and laid the identical pattern and size of fly, No. 12 Dr. Breck, across the same rock. The tug came immediately, but this time I was prepared to yield to it. The leader held, and in time we laid on the moss a gorgeous sixteen-inch male fish, a perfect model of an Adirondack squaretail, with the two flies side by side in its upper jaw.

Between the two small pockets were long stretches of beautiful fast-moving water strewn with logs and large boulders and full of crayfish and insect life needed to sustain a large trout population. Although trout were present in the spring, all through the summer neither we nor anybody else could find one. There were similar fine stretches above Buttermilk Falls all the way to Forked Lake and in the river above between Forked and Raquette. More than once we tried to persuade the Fish and Game people to stock the river with browns and rainbows so that this water might hold trout during the summer. The answer from Albany was no. The upper Raquette River was one of the few large systems left in the state with water of a quality to support brook trout and it should be kept for that species. We were on the point of ordering browns and rainbows from a private hatchery and stocking the river ourselves, but on reflection we decided not to interfere with the state's program which was based on scientific study and had behind it the great tradition of the region—even if, as Bige said, "Thar wa'n't no law against it." We remembered the case of Rob Shaw and Lysander Hall. They too probably thought they were doing a great thing for the lake when they dumped their tub full of pike in the weed beds at the edge of town, with no more idea than a pair of babes of the frightful mischief they were doing to the native squaretails.

23

Approaching the Big Pool below Raquette Lake, water at midsummer level.

Clint Sutton and Jim Flynn had often told us that if we yearned to catch trout in the river we should come in May, the earlier the better, and not later than the first week of June. Of course the early fishing was all done with spinners and bait, but by May 20 we could expect some fly fishing. I got there only once at the right time, and then only for an afternoon. We had driven up over Decoration Day weekend to plant the garden and arrange to have everything in order for the summer. Saturday was a brilliant day, the air crisp and exhilarating. I took off around two o'clock for the river and fished down from the bridge below Raquette Lake. Sure enough, there were trout in the same runs where I had taken bass in low water the summer before. The river was still up from weeks of rain, and they were lying deep. In the racing flood it was useless to cast directly at the target or even ten feet above it. I had to cast well upstream to allow the fly to sink and drift past me, dropping deeper as it went. When all worked right, that is, when I was able to hang the fly deep and at the right spot beside a log or rock, I caught a trout or at least saw one make a dash at the fly, and that was exciting, too.

After an hour of this I came around a bend and saw the current rushing into a wide pool through which it moved smoothly and swiftly for about three hundred feet. With such a vast amount of water it looked completely unfamiliar, although I had fished here many times before. This had to be the pool that Jim and Clint talked about, where salmon and trout from both Raquette and Forked Lakes congregated in the high waters of early spring.

Along the way I had seen large winged ants crawling out of the streamside logs and driftwood. Now as I looked for a place from which to fish the pool, some of these ants appeared flying about me, a few at first and then quickly more until they filled the air. They looked as big as the large stone flies of midsummer, and their wings made the same greyish blur. Many were over the river, some flying low to the water, falling into it, and spinning about with buzzing wings as they tried to get airborne again. There was a heavy splash out in the pool and then another. Soon fish of a size that I saw only once in many years were smashing away at the tumbling ants. There were no quiet rises, all

Netting one in the Big Pool below Raquette Lake.

hard smashes. Some appeared to be salmon, but I saw enough color to know that there were large trout among them.

I waded out. My side of the river was ordinarily a low bank of sand and gravel, the practical side from which to fish. But today the sand was covered, the river had risen into the trees, and where I stepped into it the water came to my hips. I went out to the top of my waders, and still I was only a few feet out from the bank and the wall of trees behind me—room for a short back cast but not enough to reach those fish far out on the flooded river. Nor was the roll cast adequate. I tried, but my best efforts were short. What I needed was a boat, a pier, or about two more feet of height. A man eight or nine feet tall might have done just fine. I went back upriver to the bridge, crossed over, and came down the other side. Here the water was so deep at the bank that I could not step into it at all. So I went back via the bridge to my first position, by which time the flight of ants was over, with only an occasional straggler falling to the water. The action had lasted perhaps an hour. I stayed at the pool hoping for a repetition until late in the day, but it did not come, and I went away leaving behind me more really large fish than I have seen before or since in one concentration. Frustrating, yes, but next day the frustration has no importance. It is all part of the game, and the sight of those swirling, splashing big ones had its own value and delight. After more than forty years, the memory is vivid still.

The Boys of Big Brook

THE CEDAR RIVER was another large stream that we sometimes fished for both trout and bass. In its lower reaches, and for several miles above its meeting with the Hudson, it was a stately river, winding through a park-like wildnerness, and could only be fished from the canoe. Higher up it could be waded, and there were meadow stretches that could be fished from the bank. In the meadows half a mile below the highway was a spring hole from which we often took both trout and bass on the same day, and when we were through, the guide fishing with a worm could take a small mess of bullheads. The summer visitor might prefer trout for the table, but the choice of every Adirondack woodsman was the bullhead. Occasionally we ventured beyond the Cedar to the Indian River country.

"Boys," Guy Saint-Marie, the pharmacist at Indian Lake village would say, "the brown trout are in there as long as my arm. I've never been able to catch one, I don't know anyone who can tell you how, but if you think you can do it, don't pass it up. Now I'm telling you—as long as my arm"—and Saint Marie had an arm like a cedar post. We never encountered one of his giants, but the farmer who lived at the mouth of the Indian confirmed the story. In the fall of 1934, he said, a deer hunter coming by at a time of low water in the pool where the Indian flows into the Hudson shot one that weighed some fifteen pounds. We had no reason to doubt him, much, for it is big water—big enough to be the home of monsters, although the few trout and bass we rose there were small fish.

One day of pouring rain, finding the Indian swollen beyond recognition, we headed for higher ground, and some miles above Indian Lake found a little meadow stream that looked fishable. While I stood in the rain, stringing up my rod, two boys piled out of a nearby farmhouse and rolled down the road on a little wagon they had made by wiring a plank to some go-cart wheels.

"Ought to be a good day for a big brown trout, mister."

They had lost a dandy yesterday under the bridge, a great big one. And what had they hooked him on?

"Nightcrawler. That's the best bait for these old browns."

My silver-bodied bucktail was approved, however, and so was the rest of the tackle after they had examined it, tested the leader knot, and held the rod—all of this before I was allowed to go down to the stream. Thus I met Lynn and Lee McCane, two years out of Schenectady but already as much at home in the mountains as a couple of young Mohawks.

They stood beside me firing questions as I fished. They hoped I would catch a good one "on that rod." They wanted to know if I liked pickerel fishing, if I liked bullhead fishing. I liked all fishing. They did, too. They would rather fish than eat. They knew a little brook where they could get the limit of twenty-five small trout (but legal, mister) any day; they knew a pond in the woods full of pickerel, big ones, ten-pounders—did I fish for pickerel with plugs? Yes, did they? Well they did not have any. I said that I would bring them up some plugs.

Well, they knew another pond where there were brown trout. On their uncle's farm. They would take me there. When would I come again? Nobody could fish the pond but their uncle's friends. What kind of fishing did we have in Washington? Is fishing tackle cheaper in Washington than it is up here? Yes, it is. They thought it must be.

"Plain old ring hooks are penny apiece up here."

I said I had some extra hooks and gut I would bring them next time.

"Gee, mister, cast over there. You see that swirly place? Big rock under there. A dandy big brown trout's under the rock. We seen him lots of times."

My bucktail seemed lost in the muddied water. I wished aloud that I had a minnow. Lee reached down with cupped hands and scooped a minnow from the water where it overflowed the grassy bank. Just like that. All I had to do was ask. I hooked the minnow through the back fin— they approved of that—and flipped it toward the eddy by the rock.

"Hold your breath," said Lynn.

"Now," said Lee, "just about another second," as the line came past the rock and held for a moment while two feet down the bait circled in a vortex. "Man, that will bring him out."

"Try it again. Put her just where you did the first time."

"That's it. Tease him a little. Let him see it again."

"Gee, mister, I bet you catch the biggest brown trout ever was caught in Big Brook."

By now they had me as tense as they were. "He's right behind that rock," said Lee. "That's where he's got to be in all this water."

"Got to be."

"He'll see that minnie next time."

"Boy when he does, watch out!"

I repeated the drift.

"It's just a matter of time," said Lynn.

"Keep that bait in the water," said Lee. Nobody ever had harder working cheerleaders.

Ed Wallace came out of the car during a lull in the downpour and fished around the bridge downstream. The rain came down again. Ed rushed back to the car.

"He don't like to fish much, does he?"

"Yes he does, but he didn't bring his raincoat."

"We didn't neither. We don't have one."

Ed comes out again as the rain stops. A boy goes over to him.

"You don't like to fish much, do you mister?"

The rain begins again and Ed runs back to the car. It is a cloudburst this time. I say, "Why don't you boys get in the car with Ed? You're getting drenched out here. You'll catch cold."

"Naw, this ain't nothing. Do us good."

I would give a lot to coax a good brown trout out to gratify these boys, but the fine silvery minnow, like the bucktail, does not produce.

Would they like to go back to Schenectady?

"Naw."

As we drive away they are running like deer through the rain, waving goodbye, leaving the little cart behind.

I went back there with Bop a week or so later. The boys were nowhere in sight, but I had hardly strung the rod

31

Camp scene: fly-tying preparations for the day's fishing were often complicated.

and tied on a fly when Lynn ran down the road from the house. He was eating a large hunk of chocolate cake, and it looked good. A five-year-old brother whose peeling face was striped with bands of pink and sickly brown, came trailing after him. Lynn said, "Go back to the house and tell Lee the fishermen are here." Shortly Lee was with us and little brother too. They brought a can full of night-crawlers, but the water today was low and clear, and I said I would stick with the fly.

"Try a Black Gnat," said Lynn. Since nothing was showing anyway, I did.

"Better put on a Beaverkill now," said Lee.

"Black Gnat's the best damn fly there is," said Lynn.

" 'Tain't in it with a Beaverkill," said Lee.

"Brown Hackle's good too."

"So's Coachman. That's maybe the best."

"Hell it is. Ain't in it with a Black Gnat."

We fished through the big pool at the bridge and then up the right fork, changing flies as Lynn or Lee had another hunch. Meanwhile Bop had gone downstream with the wet fly. As we fished through the meadow, Lynn told little brother to go on home now, because the sun was too hot for him and he would get sunburned all over again. Besides, he was in the way. But little brother would not go. The rock where the big brown is said to live was well above water today. Lynn pointed to the ripple above it, and told me to cast there.

"But try this side of the rock first," said Lee, which was good advice, too. I cautioned them to stay well back or their shadows would frighten the trout. Lynn saw to it that his brothers did, but he, himself, with my net, crept nearer and sat in the grass beside me.

I know there must be a big brown near the rock for

their enthusiasm cannot be invented. But again I could not interest him, and at last the boys gave up on me and went downstream to see what Bop was doing.

Lynn is tow headed, blue eyed, lean, and tall for his eleven years and carries himself very straight. Highly strung, impulsive. Asks questions in a stream, but without sequence. "Ever been to Cedar River House? Can you tie a fly? Can you cook over a fire? Want to buy some blueberries? You like sweet butter?" Lee, ten, is shorter than Lynn, dark haired, dark eyed, and slight of build. He is quieter than his brother but equally sure of himself—if anything, more positive.

They found Bop on the brook below the bridge and talked him into going to Round Lake for the rest of the day, since Big Brook was not producing. They also sold him a gallon of blueberries and two pounds of sweet butter. Their story on Round Lake is that it is full of big bass—up to five pounds—and off the mouth of Sucker Brook are big trout—up to three and four. Little brother was dragged kicking to the house and we started for Round Lake, by car to the Chimney Mountain House, and then by trail through the woods a mile or more. At a fork in the trail there was loud argument between Lynn and Lee, Lynn holding out for the left fork and Lee for the right. We settled the matter by splitting off with them—Bop with Lynn and Lee with me. On the way Lee pointed out seven different kinds of wild animal dung—squirrel, rabbit, fox, coon, deer, bear, and "porcapine." I took his word for it. We were at the boat landing in twenty-five minutes. Five minutes later Bop and Lynn came down the shoreline. Bop went off in a boat to try the bass, while the boys led me to the mouth of Sucker Brook. Small trout were rising there, and I soon caught two six- or seven-inchers. The boys reviled me for putting them back, so when another took the fly I did not try to hook it. But the quiet rise was followed by an imposing swirl, and I got the rod back only in time to feel a little tick as the hook came away.

"You asleep there, Vincent?" asked Lynn. "Goddam that was a buster."

"We told you they was big ones in here," said Lee. "You got to be on your toes."

I was sick about this, both for losing the trout and for letting the boys down, and when another small spat appeared on the surface I was ready and came back quick and hard. Of course the leader broke and there was another imposing swirl. "God damyou, Vincent, what in hell's a matter with you?" Two vexed faces were turned to me and both voices rose.

This was too good to keep, and on the trail back, with the boys scrambling through the woods on the trail of a chipmunk, I told the story to Bop. He tried to pump them. "What kind of a fisherman is Vincent?"

"He throws the fly all right," said Lee, "but he don't catch much."

"Good field, no hit, you mean," suggested Bop.

"He almost had coupla big ones just the same," said Lynn. My chest swelled at this sign of loyalty until he added, "wisht *I* had the rod."

Sudden leaping and lunging away down the trail. "Goddam porcapine." Through the ferns we saw the black low shape, the aura of grey quills, the nearsighted turning of the head, the blundering movement toward safety.

"Get a club."

"Sock him."

35

Pete Engels with his first Long Lake fish (he took it to bed with him that night).

Lee stopped to break off a dead sapling. Lynn was already pounding with a small stick. The animal got to a big tree, circled it, and began to climb.

"Got in one good hit anyway," said Lynn. "Wisht we had a .22."

Lee is almost as excited. "Goddam porcapines, they kill more timber than anything in the woods."

We tell them the porcupines are protected by law,

36

and why. They look thoughtful and are subdued for a change, as if they felt rebuked.

"Just the same if you was lost and starving, bet you'd never see one," said Lee.

"That's right," said Lynn; "they'd all be up the trees."

Boiling Pond and
a Dancing Hermit

Fishing a pond in midsummer began with a search for the spring holes. Finding them did not mean that you were about to fill the boat; all other factors that make for luck had to be in conjunction, too. I recall a day on Handsome Pond that began with such a flourish we stopped fishing while the fun was at its height in order to save some of it for tomorrow. We should have made the most of it and then gone home, for next day there were no fish to be found anywhere. Another year Mr. Emery and Clint Sutton came back from several days at Grassy Pond with fourteen squaretail trout, eight or nine of which weighed from two pounds to more than four. An estimated five-pounder had been lost when it tumbled from the net. I went back with them the following year under the same phase of the moon and identical conditions of weather and water. Two days we spent at the spring holes with no luck at all. Even Clint was blanked, still fishing for our supper with his Black Gnat, flavor added. I found some blueberries on a rocky slope and I went swimming, so the trip was not a waste of time. But what trip to the wilderness ponds ever is?

At Moose Pond, beyond the Anthonys, it was a

guide that betrayed us. Clint Sutton was guiding out of the Sagamore just then, and Ed Wallace had not yet come into our lives. We hired a guide—to spare the feelings of his descendants we will refer to him as Tuffy—to take us in for an overnight stay. He had been recommended to us by Lahey's Store in Long Lake because his grocery bill was hopelessly overdue. Tuffy lost his way, and we sat on a log beside our pack baskets while the rain poured down in buckets and he circled about looking for the trail. For a time we heard him crashing through the brush, now on this side, now on that. Then all was silence except for the rain on the leaves and a far-off roll of thunder. We went looking for Tuffy and found him on what was obviously the wrong side of the ridge, still circling. We were all afternoon getting to Moose Pond, only four miles through the woods, and fell into the lean-to thoroughly bushed but cheered by a break in the clouds and the prospect of good weather for tomorrow.

"Bad beginning, good ending," said Tuffy, and it seemed he might be right.

Perhaps because we had been so tired, we slept late the next morning—we did not wake until six o'clock. There was a lovely golden light on the water and a blue sky overhead, but no fire and no guide. We assumed he was in the woods looking for a cedar stump to knock apart for kindling. But then we went down to the landing to wash up and found the boat was gone. Shouts and whistles, no response. Where could he be, we asked each other. We had the fire going and breakfast well under way when our guide came rowing in.

"You fellers were asleep," he said, "so thought I'd just do some fishing." He had thirty-seven trout in the boat.

While my groans sent the deermice scurrying for

cover, Bop said mildly, "Well, you have covered yourself with glory, I must say. You have also ruined the spring hole for us and broken the law by taking so many trout."

Tuffy said, "But we're entitled to twenty-five apiece and I'm just helping you get your limit. Just trying to be a good feller."

We left him to get his own breakfast and took the boat ourselves. No trout offered at the spring hole, but the place was alive with tiny sunfish. We rowed all around the shores looking for another likely spot, and along the way we caught a thousand three-inch sunfish. Several times an amusing otter passed close to the boat, swimming about three feet under the water on his back. Forty yards ahead of us he surfaced and looked back, then repeated the maneuver. Perhaps he thought we were throwing back the sunfish for his benefit, but more likely he was showing off.

"Bad beginning, worse ending," said Bop to Tuffy when we paid him off. The following summer I heard that Tuffy had been saying that he would like to guide Mr. Emery again, but not "that boy." "That boy" was myself, then thirty years of age. Mr. Emery, he said, was a fine gentleman but "that boy" had a wicked temper and didn't appreciate what a feller was trying to do for him.

These ponds—Handsome, Grassy, the Anthonys, and Moose—where the trout lay in spring holes through the summer were all at around seventeen hundred feet of altitude. Lost Pond and Boiling Pond on Mt. Seward were very much higher, and here the fish were not so concentrated within small areas. There were places that they favored and places where we ordinarily did not expect to find them, but any place that had cover was worth a try. The fishing here was from rafts that rode awash. Each had been provided with a seat made of a box nailed to the middle logs, so we fished all day in comfort. We wore strong leather boots—not to keep our feet dry, because they did not, but for protection from leeches that might swim aboard. Boiling Pond had more leeches per cubic foot of water than Moose Pond had sunfish. Perhaps for this reason Boiling Pond trout were slimmer for their length than the trout of other Adirondack ponds and slow-flowing streams. Of the waters we fished, Brandreth Stream had the chunkiest and heaviest trout in proportion to length, then came Grassy and Lake Colden, about equal in this respect, and at the bottom of the list was Boiling Pond. This puzzled us. We assumed that a diet which no doubt included a high percentage of leeches could not be very fattening. Yet growth was permitted, for the trout of Boiling Pond were longer than we had expected to find in such a small body of water, no wider or deeper than many a beaver pond. We caught many twelve to fourteen inches long, a few of fifteen to sixteen, and one of seventeen. That longest fish, although obviously in health and vigor, scarcely weighed two pounds. The same fish from Brandreth Stream would have been three-quarters of a pound heavier.

When fishing Boiling Pond, we stayed at the old logging dam on Cold River. Our host was a pleasant man of the woods named Noah Rondeau, later to become widely known as "the hermit of the Adirondacks." Webster defines a hermit as "a person who retires from society and lives in solitude, especially from religious motives; recluse; anchorite." Mr. Rondeau was clearly a recluse, but although he was reading *The Western Christian Messenger* when I first came upon him, he was no more a hermit of the devotional type than Natty Bumppo or Henry David Thoreau. He lived in the woods because he loved nature and detested the towns, and particularly the presence in the towns of people who might set limits to his independence—mayors, sheriffs, and the administrators of the fish and game laws. At four

Cold River below Rondeau's camp, site of old dam for floating logs.
New York State Department of Environmental Conservation.

points in the woods marking the minimal limits of what he considered his domain, he had carved on the logs and painted on the rocks this notice—

> *Earl A. Vosburgh is an American thief.*
> *Ray J. Burgomaster is an American liar.*
> [Signed] N. J. Rondeau.

The same proclamation had been affixed to his cabin door.

Messrs. Vosburgh and Burgomaster were game protectors. Mr. Rondeau accused the first of stealing fur from his traps. Back in the thirties the state did occasionally recruit a case-hardened game violator as a warden. It was one way to get him out of the business, and who better equipped to deal with other poachers than a man who knew the ropes? Vosburgh, said Mr. Rondeau, was such a man except that he had not reformed, at least not completely. For example, one winter Mr. Rondeau had cause to suspect that a two-legged animal was pilfering his trap line. So one day when he found a nice mink in the set along Cold River he left it there and hid himself in the brush to watch. Vosburgh came along, found the mink, and was taking it from the trap when Rondeau sprang from ambush, gun at the ready, backed him up against a tree, and vowed instant execution if he should be found anywhere in this territory again. At least that was the story in 1934. Ed Wallace informed me that the details were embellished as time went on, but essentials remained the same. And every year on the anniversary of this confrontation, Mr. Rondeau went twenty miles on snowshoes to mail a post card reminding Game Protector Vosburgh that he was not an honest man.

Mr. Burgomaster's offense was even more serious. He had doubted the authenticity and validity of the scrap of wrapping paper on which the head of the lumbering firm of Meigs and Meigs had scrawled a deed, giving the hermit title to the camp buildings and the ground on which they stood. So he brought Mr. Rondeau into court, charging him with maintaining a permanent camp on state forest lands. The court found the paper good, however, and Mr. Burgomaster went down in the books as an American liar. He, too, received an anniversary post card.

Another time should Vosburgh or Burgomaster trespass upon the hermitage, Rondeau would be ready for them. Daily he practiced with the bow and arrow, his target the outline of a warden's hat. The bow had been covered with narrow strips of beaver hide, wound on while still green and then allowed to dry and shrink in place. It had a pull of seventy-five pounds. The wicked-looking arrow heads had been hacked and filed by Rondeau himself from the blade of a cross-cut saw, then soldered into a brass cartridge case and fitted to the end of the shaft. We were invited to try the bow. I could not hold it steady when pulled to full arrow length myself, although I was taller, heavier, and younger than Mr. Rondeau. Ed Wallace, who was as brawny as a fullback, could handle it, but his shots went wild. It was child's play for Rondeau, who sent arrow after arrow into the hat. He consoled us by saying that if we practiced with him daily, we would no doûbt work up to it—in time.

The bow had advantages for one who must live in and with the woods, he found. He could kill deer and partridge without the report of the .30-.30 shattering the silence and frightening other game. It was a great weapon for defense against interlopers, too. His sweetest dream was of nailing Vosburgh's hat to a tree with a well-placed arrow.

"And if the shot happens to strike a bit low, that will be too bad, eh? Nothing planned or deliberate, of course. Weather affects the bow's performance—it could be a trifle off that day. Or there just *might* be a suggestion from the subconscious. A reflex you could not control. Like this, maybe. Oh, oh, poor shot, that. Too bad." He did a little jig.

"How sad. What a terrible thing."

He was called a hermit, but he enjoyed company. We had carried with us a new lightweight tent—complete

Left to right: Ed Wallace, Noah J. Rondeau at target practice, James A. Emery.

with sewed-in ground cloth and mosquito netting, and large enough for three men—intending to set it up on the grassy flat beside the dam. Ed suggested that we first pay our respects to Mr. Rondeau, whose camp was on the high ground above, and ask permission, which we did.

"But of course, of course," he said, "go right ahead. But I have a better idea. Stay here with me."

There were two log cabins in the yard, all that remained of the logging camp of Meigs and Meigs. The cabin he now occupied had been the camp office. The other, which he moved to when winter came, had been the sleeping quarters of the camp boss and very important visitors. The Meigs themselves had often slept in it. We must move into this commodious cabin. He assured us it was weather tight, and we believed him. Its logs would have withstood cannon. One could not find such mammoth timbers anywhere today.

We said we could not think of it. We had hauled our tent a long way, eleven miles from the foot of the lake by way of Shattuck Clearing, and said we were anxious to try it out. What we really had in mind was what would happen to us when all was dark and the mosquitoes came out from the crevices in those log walls, and from beneath the broken chairs and benches piled in the corners, and from behind the rags of clothing hanging from the walls. We had left our blood in abandoned camps and lean-tos before this when forced by a thunderstorm to take shelter, and that was the reason we now packed a tent. Besides, the weather was warm, and the tiny windows and one narrow door of the cabin did not promise much in the way of ventilation. Ventilation was the very thing they had been constructed to prevent. At thirty degrees below zero, no matter how tightly you build the cabin, you have all the ventilation you can use. But this was mid-July, the time of hot weather.

The yard had been described to us by the envious at Shattuck's Clearing as a pig pen, which was unfair and untrue. It was a wolf's den, hard and dry, and the bones and skulls of small animals and fishes lay scattered about, with bits of hide around which gathered the hornets and bluebottle flies. At the side of the yard tall poles had been brought together teepee fashion and chained at the top, and from the center of this arrangement hung chains with hooks attached. One hook now held a large iron kettle. At sundown that evening, and for the several evenings of our stay, we were to have a trout chowder from that kettle, seasoned with saffron like the bouillabaisse of the Marseilles fishing boats and just as good.

We said no, no thanks, we would use the tent and thought that had settled it. Bop and Ed Wallace went off to try Boiling Pond. I stayed behind, for my feet were in no shape to travel another mile that day. I was wearing new boots and my heels had blistered and worn raw on the pine needle trails, which were slippery from weeks of dry warm weather. Mr. Rondeau said it was a shame I had come so far only to sit around the camp, why did I not try the still-water above the dam, there were big squaretails under the spirea. He used to keep a boat there, but it had disappeared one day; he thought perhaps some hikers had taken it up-river and left it there. He would go look for it now, but he had work to do.

"So why not try your luck from the bank for an hour or two?" I said it was too hot and bright and perhaps too late in the year to fish stillwater; the river looked dead to me.

"Yes, that it does. But sometimes the unexpected happens. Then we call it luck. Why don't you give your luck a run? See what happens?"

His smile was so encouraging, his sympathy so unaffected, I felt ashamed and said, "You're right. I'll put my rod together." He had me take off my boots and brought me a pair of moccasins, oiled and worn until they were the color of the ground, soft as butter on the feet. I crossed the dam as ordered and fished from the other bank, so that I could cast toward the spirea. Shortly Mr. Rondeau came by carrying an axe and a tarpaulin. I heard him chopping away on the hill behind me, and then he was back, walking slowly and bent over with an enormous load of balsam on his back.

"Hard times," he called to me with a smile. I watched him labor up the steep bank toward the cabins and knew that mosquitoes or no mosquitoes, we could not sleep in our new tent this night.

I fished until the sky was red behind the hills. Several times a cloud of minnows went skittering over the water and I thought a big trout must be chasing them. But then I realized that it was only my bucktail fly that frightened them, darting out from the other bank as I retrieved.

Mr. Rondeau was pulling carrots from the garden when I returned. He had half a bucket of small potatoes, too, no bigger than hickory nuts, from the vines that I saw competing with the weeds. My luck was bad, he said, but at least I had given it a try. The red gods would think better of me for that. Now we would make a stew for we would all be mighty hungry men by dark.

Bop and Ed came back about then with eight or nine trout, including a fifteen-incher that Rondeau seized and held up by the tail as he did an Indian dance around the fire. Their luck, he said, was great. He was looking more like a character from Fenimore Cooper every minute, the fire glinting red on his pointed features and casting his shadow enormously on the mist rising from the river.

In the morning he anointed my blisters with a salve made of bear fat and the mashed leaves of wintergreen. He assured me it would heal. There were two doctors from New York City who came to fish with him every spring, and he had given it to them when they showed up with bruises and blisters. They said it would probably not work in New York but was great up here.

"Medicine must be like fishing, eh?" he said. "Some skill, some faith, and a lot of luck. Luck is the important thing. Of course I don't know about medicine but there are no fixed rules that are any good in fishing. Like the French language there are only exceptions."

Ed went off to scout some small ponds that Mr. Rondeau had told us about, while Bop and I fished Boiling Pond. It looked as quiet and dead as the stillwater on Cold River except for the leeches that investigated the raft and the trout that swirled around the fly. We brought back nothing but big fish that day, fourteen to seventeen inches long, and Mr. Rondeau said our luck was unbelievable.

I used to hear from him in the winter, usually after New Year's Day. He would write that he had been 342 days in the woods since his last trip to town. In October he had seen a young bear crossing Cold River below the dam. There were lots of beech nuts this fall, which had been good for the deer. He had killed five partridge with the bow and arrow, knocking them out of the tree one at a time. One would fall and the others would sit there, preferring not to risk a flight that might take them into greater danger. He was expecting the two doctors from New York around the end of May. Probably they would make him shave his beard again, but that was the only change they would allow him to make. Particularly they did not want any tidying up around the camp—cleanup was what they were trying to get away from, two weeks in the year. "I will oblige them in this, as they are real Mohawks at heart, and my good friends." And he would close by inviting us to return to the old dam and catch the big fish under the spirea. Below his signature would be a sketch of the dam and the big trout poised in the stillwater.

Brandreth Stream

BRANDRETH STREAM comes down to the western arm of Forked Lake through bog and marsh land, half hidden among the tall reeds and cattails, with alder brush and cranberries growing from the hummocks, and nothing higher except the weathered skeletons of a few dead pines and tamaracks. The water is cold and good but appears dark because of the silty bottom. The flow is smooth, streaming the water weeds and gurgling around old snags. Bass wander up from the lake now and then, and usually there are perch about. But the prize of the river is its trout—deep-bellied, chunky fish, dark as anthracite, with jewelled spots. Back in the thirties it was little fished, although occasionally we met Clint Sutton or a Whitney guide there. If his sport was not a skilled fly fisher, Clint would row him slowly up and down the lower water, dragging a spinner and fly behind the boat. Or he would anchor and have the man still fish with a worm at the point of a black fly. Many a two-pound trout he took from the river this way.

As word of a good thing spreads rapidly, and a little river like Brandreth could not accommodate many fishermen, we held its secret close. However, I once took a friend

Forked Lake, looking west from the head of Long Carry. *Photo by Edward Bierstadt. Adirondack Museum, Blue Mountain Lake, New York.*

there who was up for a short visit and could be trusted not to talk. This friend had done some trout fishing in the tumbling brooks of Maryland but had never fished quiet water, and the first sight of the inlet did nothing for his courage. "Is *this* the stream?"

"This is it."

"I suppose it runs faster higher up?"

"Up in the green timber, yes."

"Is that where we are going?"

"Maybe later, if we don't get anything here."

Charlie's voice got throaty. "This does not look like a *trout stream* to me!"

"Why not? What don't you like about it?"

"The streams we fished in Maryland are full of waterfalls and foam and you know when you see them that they're just *full* of trout. They are so beautiful! It gives you confidence just to look at them."

I said, "Quiet now, Charlie. We'll try it in this bend. Take a hold of that grass and we'll ease the boat into it."

The water was shallow on this side, but near the opposite bank it flowed six feet deep beneath the high bush cranberries.

"There's our pool. You take the lower end, and I'll take the upper."

Charlie looked over his flies and picked out a Black Gnat. I told him to let it settle deep. His first cast produced a small perch. He drew it close to the boat and let it swim around there. He talked to it. He said, "What do you and I know about trout streams?"

He cast out again and something else took hold; he struck it hard and lost the fly. I said, "There's your proof. There went a good trout."

"I don't believe you," said Charlie. "More likely it was a pretty fair bass."

I cast in turn and saw a flash of white beneath the fly. The sun was out now, and the leader glittered in the quiet water. That probably had been the trouble. I took it in, rubbed it with mud and said, "They're in here, Charlie. We should get some fishing by and by."

The fish would not come a second time, and I decided to save him for later. We slid upstream to the next

53

bend where the stream moves deeply between an alder clump and a grassy point. I cast into the tail of this pool; a fish swirled and I felt his weight as I snubbed.

"Another bass," said Charlie.

He was a strong fish. I could not keep him out of the pool. He rolled on the surface and I thought I had him, but he went down again stronger than ever. Then he rolled at the surface again, and I saw that he was hooked in one of the frontal fins. When Charlie netted him the whole net glowed from the color of that trout. When the fish had been taken out, the mesh returned to its faded mauve. All along the belly of the fish was the bright iridescent purple which the *fontinalis* take on as autumn and the spawning time approach. We thought it better than fifteen inches in length, but on the tape at home it measured a scant fourteen and a half. It weighed one and a half pounds even, however. Such weight for length would be unheard of in a trout of the running brooks but is about average for the squaretails of Brandreth Stream.

We fished on up the stream, pulled the guideboat over an old beaver dam, and went on to a second dam, taking some small fish on the way. At the second dam we had our sandwiches and beer and rested, waiting for evening.

A canoe appeared around the bend upstream, paddled by a young couple. They were from the camping grounds at Clear Pond (now Lake Eaton) near Long Lake. They had fishing gear with them—short plugging rods and a large tackle box—and had gone up into the green timber looking for a trout.

The man said, "I've never seen a trout. I've heard about them but I'm beginning to believe they don't exist. It's just a great beautiful myth."

The girl said, "I'd settle for a fish of any kind. We haven't seen one in three days."

I said that we just happened to have a brook trout in the boat, and held it up. The girl said, "Oh what a lovely fish."

The man said, "Well, now at least we've seen one and I can believe. That's the first step."

Charlie said, "I thought you'd show it off sooner."

"But I wanted to make certain they were not trout fishermen before I did. Did not want to encourage them to hang around."

"Nice man," said Charlie.

We fished again. Charlie had tried several flies and now put on a Scarlet Ibis, because he liked the color. He had some hits, I assumed from perch or sunfish, but perhaps not, for finally he hooked one and hauled in a seven-inch trout. It is the only fish I can remember seeing caught on the Red Ibis.

At six o'clock, we were downriver near the alder bend again. Soon I had another heavy brookie in the net.

"To hell with this," said Charlie, "If you can do it, I can too." He yanked the Red Ibis from the leader and replaced it with a black and white bucktail. He had the real medicine this time. A trout came out from the logs and hit it hard.

"I told you so," said Charlie. It was in fact the best fish yet, one pound, ten ounces. We dropped down to the bend by the cranberry bushes, and on the first cast there he had another fish. Two big trout on successive casts. Meanwhile I was doing nothing. A little later he hooked and lost a third. That ended the action.

As we drifted toward the lake, Charlie said, "Why have you been keeping this from me? It is positively the loveliest stream I ever saw. Anywhere. The marsh is so peaceful and beautiful, too. I wish I didn't have to go back tomorrow. I cannot wait until we come back to this place."

Charlie was in the hospital last Christmas time and I wrote him these few lines.

The birds have flown from Brandreth Marsh
The trout have left the redds.
Dark ice forms above them. Snow
Sifts from the overcast—
Marsh, meadow beyond, and lake
Become one snowy plain
That winding hollow, lined with brush
Tells of the stream beneath.

Though forty years have come and gone
Since we last saw the place
I could return to Brandreth Marsh
By day or even night
And place my foot upon the spot
Mounded now with snow
Where Charlie fisherman and I
Made fast our cedar boat.
—Startling the great blue heron
    And the osprey from its snag—
And, where the weed streams lakeward
Cast out our silvered flies
To lure the trout of Brandreth
An ancient mountain strain
That glow with stained glass colors
And flaming fins.

We said yes, we would be back there
When summer came again
But forty summers now have passed
And we have not returned.
While fiercely Time's eroded
Ourselves and the world we knew

But Brandreth Stream still flows as clear
As cold within its marsh.
What great good news for once it is
To hear that this remains
Where once within a bank of reeds
We hid that slender boat,
Made envious the great heron
The wheeling hawk amazed
As to the light of evening
We held the river's prize.

A Black Gnat with Flavor Added

I N THE BEGINNING we carried and used many patterns of flies. Later, 90 percent of our fishing was done with four—a bucktail with silver body and jungle cock cheeks; a small black nymph ribbed with fine silver wire; the Van Patten, an old Adirondack favorite that bears a family resemblance to the Professor; and Dr. Breck, which is in effect a Parmacheene Belle with a silver body.

It was the state ranger at Lake Colden, Clint West, who tipped us off to the Van Patten. I had noticed that he invariably fished Queen of the Waters.

"Yes," said Clint, "but if I could only find a Van Patten I would never use anything else." It had been a favorite with the Tahawus Club many years before, he said, "but I haven't seen one since before the war. I've written to dealers and I've asked everybody who comes up here, but I seem to be the only man left who ever heard of it."

Back home again the books I had did not describe it, and neither Mills nor Abercrombie carried it in their catalogs. On a hunch I wrote to Vom Hofe, who had by then moved to Philadelphia, and Vom Hofe had it, in fact carried it regularly. It had the Professor's yellow body, but

58

with a small gold tip in lieu of gold ribbing, and a wing of heavily barred black and white wood duck instead of the speckled gray mallard. A dozen were sent up to Clint West, and others came with us when we went north again the following year. It became a steady favorite, probably because of Clint West's strong recommendation and the confidence with which we therefore fished it.

The Dr. Breck we came by accidentally one day of passing showers when there was a concentration of trout among the submerged rocks off the mouth of a small brook on Handsome Pond. Several duller patterns had failed to take. We had recently been given some ten thousand flies by a friend of the family, "Uncle Jimmy" Robertson, and were running through them when we came upon this white and scarlet pattern. There was no further need to experiment for it took at once. For several hours, taking turns so as not to foul the lines, we struck fish on every other cast, beautiful dark squaretails, running from three-quarters of a pound to a pound and something over. Since we were camping at the Pond we kept only the few we needed for supper and breakfast, the rest were carefully put back. Next day would be the better time to catch and kill the fish we intended to bring home. Next day was another story, however, and we went back fishless except for the few that Clint Sutton, who was guiding us, coaxed out of a spring hole, patiently fishing his special version of a No. 6 Black Gnat on the bottom. But Dr. Breck had shown what it could do when the fish were in the mood, and we used it ever after, often to deadly effect.

While the four flies were all we really needed, like most fishermen we continued to carry and from time to time use many others. Fishing the wilderness ponds in July and August, I do not recall ever having seen an insect hatch large enough to excite the attention of the fish and keep

59

them concentrating on that one insect to the exclusion of anything else. I heard of a blizzard hatch occurring one evening in early July, but was told that the Queen of the Waters took care of it beautifully, so it was not a case of what has come to be called selective feeding. What we could expect to see at this time of year were singleton fish dimpling here and there. If the fish were not cruising, we could take them nine times out of ten with one of our four special favorites. If not, we had a variety of old dependables to fall back on—Brown Hackle, Black Gnat, Queen of the Waters, Royal and Leadwing Coachman, Montreal, Grizzly King, Reuben Wood.

I rarely see the Rube Wood referred to these days, but it was a familiar fly in the 1930s. One reason it appealed to us was that it is an Adirondack original and one of the comparatively few native patterns of the 1870s that had been inspired by a living insect. It was the creation of Reuben Wood of Syracuse, a famous angler and fly-casting champion of the period 1860–84. Mary Orvis Marbury tells us that the insect he tried to imitate was one he found in the Adirondacks. But what insect, and where in the Adirondacks? What could it have been, we wondered, but the adult phase of the male Green Drake,* with its white body, ginger hackle, speckled mallard wing, mallard stylets for the tail. I used to think that the red tip at the end of the body was a concession to the fancy of the times and the

---

* There are three or four mayflies known to some anglers as the Green Drake, to others as Shad Flies, or by the name of the waters where they hatch, for example, "Green Bay Flies." I refer here to the Green Drake identified by entomologists as *Ephemera guttulata*. The white body and mallard wing of the Reuben Wood might puzzle those to whom *Hexagenia rigida* is the Green Drake, and *H. limbata* their "Dark" Green Drake. In places, *E. varia* is also locally called Green Drake.

Reuben Wood of Syracuse, one of the great anglers who fre-
quented the Oswegatchie River and Cranberry Lake in the glorious
days of the last century. It is said that he could cast more than fifty
feet with a lancewood rod and more than a hundred feet with the
split bamboos of the day.

predilection of the brook trout for a touch of red. But was it? Needham, Traver, and Hsu see the final segment of the natural fly's abdomen as "largely bright red brown." Their description was based on insects collected from, among other places, the Oswegatchie River, which is the major inlet of Cranberry Lake. Everything fell into place when we learned that Reuben Wood often fished Cranberry and its inlets. In fact there is a stone monument to his memory at the mouth of Sucker Brook on the east shore of the lake.

When all else failed and we were hard up for fish to eat, Clint Sutton would turn to his Black Gnat with flavor added, and replenish the larder. Clint's added ingredient was the tough, reddish, end segment of a worm covering the hook point.

"You can't use a whole worm hooked in the middle or at one end like you would in a fast little brook, or in the ponds here in May and June," said Clint. "This time of year they lie there and suck the ends off and you'll never know they're around. It's summer now, the water's warm, they feel lazy and they're not going to chase it. You got to let it sink to the mud and lie there, and if you move it at all, not more than half an inch at a time. Less is even better."

Clint would sit in the middle seat of the guideboat staring at the water and fingering the line. Every now and then he would give a little jerk and the rod would bend. I have seen him take four and five fish from a spot while we with the same rig could not get a nibble from a bullhead. But if we pulled up the fly to look at it, the piece of worm would be missing half the time.

"You've got to sense it," he said. "You won't feel a tug. I try to think about the fish down there. They're looking the fly over and it looks interesting. They decide to investigate, but they're in no hurry. They're pretty well fed and not going to grab just anything. So they get close enough to smell it, and it smells pretty good. They lip it, and part of it tastes great, but they're not sure yet, something could be wrong. So they lip it again, real slow and careful, like a dog picking blackberries. All they want to get at is that little speck of taste. The rest of it is all muck and feathers, and something a little thorny too, so they drop it and away they go. You got to sense what's going on down there and pull at the right time, not a second too soon or too late."

He was an artist, that Clint. We tried it many a time when nothing else would work, but never did get the hang of it.

And while on the subject of flies, do you know that the Dark Montreal is *the* fly for bullheads? It is; it is, indeed.

To the left of the swimming beach on the southerly side of Pine Point on Long Lake, in the hollow of the elbow bend where the point thrusts out from the line of the shore, was a wet place where a few cattails and grasses grew behind a spit of rock and gravel. In early season when waters were high and Cold River was pouring its flood, against all normal river behavior, into the lake itself instead of its usual outlet, the lower Raquette River, the gravelly spit would be covered, and there was deep water in the pocket where the cattails grew. In one of these high-water times a lordly bull-head, of full nine and fifteen-sixteenths inches in extent from tip of tail to leathery snout, found its way into the pocket, and being asleep one night as the waters fell, was trapped there behind the spit of land in a foot of water or less, and when sunlight came there it was, as visible to the gaze of the passing world as a goldfish in its bowl.

This was too much for one idle good-for-nothing, who, after his morning dip and change into proper angling attire, complete with sunglasses, poplin hat, and fishing vest filled with fly boxes, returned to the beach with his split bamboo fly rod and neatly placed a No. 10 Dark Montreal fly before the bullhead's staring eyes. The bullhead rose to it in classic form, and after the prescribed heart-stopping struggle, was lifted out in a ten-dollar net, handcrafted by William Mills and Son of Adirondack ash grown on a northern slope with walnut inlay in a handle of bird's-eye maple.

Fortunately for the bullhead he had no companions in the pot hole or they would all have landed in the net and been borne to the kitchen, for it was Friday and fish were in demand. But since one bullhead for a table of twelve is scanty fare, and might even lead to unmannerly dissension, it was restored to the lake, bearing with it in dignity the Dark Montreal fly which the angler had been unable to extract without risk of serious damage to a fish for which he had only the greatest respect and admiration and which had honorably performed its role in demonstrating that despite the contrary opinion of perhaps the generality of experts in the matter, the bullhead *will* take an artificial fly—that is, of course, when properly presented and provided that the fly is a Dark Montreal. The deed having been observed by two witnesses of unimpeachable veracity, the angler was able to add to his lifetime list of fish taken on the fly one Common (although of notable size) American Bullhead, known in elevated circles as *Ameiurus americanus,* although come to think of it, this particular specimen might equally well have been *Ameiurus melas melas,* the Northern Black Bullhead. These distinctions can be exasperating at times, as every reader is aware.

The Bass of Upper Sargent

THERE IS A TANGLE of logs across the outlet brook at Upper Sargent. In the early light we see a grey black animal on the logs. It seems to be dipping in the water. We think it is a raccoon fishing or washing its food, and drift toward it in the boat, taking advantage of all possible cover. At sixty feet we see it is an old porky. He lifts his small black puzzled face to us, but does not see. He dips again into the water. He is feeding on the green water grasses that grow beside the log. He shakes himself like a dog, and the quills ripple and wave like long silky hair on a loose hide.

Paddling, with makeshift paddles, our clumsy batteau, we watch the bank closely, looking for any trickle of water that may indicate a spring where trout may lie. There are lots of smallmouth bass in the pond, and Duane has told us there are also a few large native squaretails, two- and three-pounders, maybe even bigger. Biekbehn of the State's Conservation Department says it is possible, for the Sargent Ponds were trout water at one time. As we search, one line is trolling a double copper spinner, the other a bass plug. A fly rod is in the bow ready for action should we find the spring. A moment comes when our lines cross. J. E. (Bop)

Jimmy Engels with chunky laker taken from South Pond by his grandfather, James A. Emery.

leans over to untangle them, and as he does I say, "I dreamed of this happening last night, in every detail. Or else I'm dreaming now." He says, "Maybe it was that coffee you made when we got up. I'm in a fog from it myself." He tells this story.

Years before when he hunted in the west, he was camped on Mount Tamalpais with his friend, George Knox. One night George dreamed that he was riding over a mountain pass. The trail was narrow, and as he reached the top a tall, red-bearded man on a gray horse was coming up from the other side. George wondered how they should get by each other on that narrow ledge without dismounting, and he woke up before he had the answer. He and Bop laughed about it at breakfast, saddled their horses, and rode off. The trail led them up the mountain. George reached the head of a pass and went down the other side out of view. Bop, following, came to the top just as a lean, tall, red-bearded man on a gray horse arrived from the other side. Down the trail George was waiting.

"Was that your man?" asked Bop.

"My man exactly," said George.

"Well how did you get by?" asked Bop.

"I dismounted," said George, "and you?"

"You set him a good example," said Bop. "He returned the favor."

At seven-thirty we come upon a good rowboat, with oars in place, pulled up in plain sight on a rocky spit. We assume this must be the boat Duane told us to use, and we swap.

With such an easy boat to handle we stop trolling and begin to cast. I row and Bop takes up the fly rod and casts with a bucktail streamer toward the shoreline. This shore of the pond is lined with the whitened snags of pines that were toppled in a great wind storm twenty years ago. Some of the main stems—two to three feet in diameter at the shore line—lie sixty feet out into the pond, at which point their tops disappear in the depths. From some a large broken limb sticks up above the surface. From beside each of these huge logs, without exception, a bass charges out and nails the fly. All are hooked, but most of them slip off as they turn back to the snag or leap into the air. Nevertheless, we take three bass of two to two and a half pounds from the bay of snags. Eight or nine more, some of them larger, have been on the hook. Past the snags we come to a weedy shallow shoreline. Action is fast here, a fish on every cast, but they are half-pounders and are returned.

Around ten o'clock action slows and we go back to the tent for breakfast. A bass is split and broiled over the coals, with strips of bacon on top to keep it moist. As we finish eating, two men come up, one a stockily built chap. He grabs the painter of the boat. "That your stuff in there?" His voice is loud.

"It is. Are you a friend of Duane's?"

"No," emphatically.

"That's Duane's boat, isn't it?"

"It is *not!* That is *my* boat!"

We explain how we found it and happened to take it. He accepts everything we say, but with heavy sarcasm; his voice trembles, his face twitches, he seems spoiling for a fight.

"You saved me a walk around the lake but I won't pay you for *that.*" He winks as he says this, not because he intends to be friendly but to show that he is on to us. He looks mad as hell. "It's a lot better boat than Duane's," and he winks again, so maybe it is a tic.

As he will be rowing back across the lake, we invite ourselves aboard in order to pick up our old batteau. I want to smoke as we go along, and feel for my pipe. Not there. We approach the rocky point where we found the boat and I see my pipe on the rock. "There it is now."

"You got pipes on all these rocks? I saw it before

you did. Thought it might give me a clue as to who took the boat before you *found* it."

His companion grins sheepishly but says nothing. Perhaps he is shy. Or maybe he knows who borrowed the boat and does not care to say.

We paddle the old batteau back to camp, rebuild the fire, and have coffee. We are heavy eyed now, having been out since first daylight, and stretch out for a nap that lasts several hours. Meanwhile the sky clouds over and there is a sprinkle of rain on the canvas that wakes us. Looking out, we see it dimpling the quiet lake.

Ed Wallace comes rowing up in Duane's boat that he found hidden in the brush near the end of the trail. An idiot could have found it, said Ed, if he had looked. Ed has carried in a pail of minnows from Long Lake. We say there is no need for minnows the way these bass are hitting the fly. Ed says, "Then I'll use them myself; goddam it, I didn't carry them in here for nothing."

We go back to the bay of snags now, Ed rowing. Fishing should be great in this pleasant shower, but not a bass comes from beneath the logs. It is hard to believe, after the performance of the morning. Ed says not a word but looks amused. The rain stops and we cross to the shore of weeds. Nothing there either. Ed rows out toward the island and anchors in fourteen feet of water.

"Well now, fly fishermen," he says, baits up with a live minnow, and almost immediately has a bass leaping into the air. When he gets another on the line we follow suit. The bass are good at stealing minnows, or we do not have the knack of it. We do not hook all that hit by any means.

Late in the afternoon, drifting back toward the landing, I hook my best fish of the day. Ed nets it and takes out the hook. He turns to drop the fish in the bow where he has

Ed Wallace of Long Lake.

a nest of green ferns and grass, the fish wriggles loose, and falls back into the lake. My back is turned to this, but I hear the splash and say, "Here's hoping it's Ed."

From Ed, "You guys have caught enough, I won't let you keep any more." We cuss him and he cusses us back.

"Next time dammit, you fly fishermen carry your own minnows down the goddam trail."

We hide Duane's boat in the brush where any idiot can find it, have a thimbleful or two sitting beside the spring, and laugh at each other as we take turns telling the other two off.

A Tupper Lake Idyll

IT RAINED HEAVILY all through the night and early morning. Around ten, looking at the sodden garden, the clearing sky, Ed said the streams would be swollen and too roily for trout, but it would be a good day to try for walleyed pike in Tupper Lake. It was Thursday, and we would need fish for Friday dinner. The ladies of the house said for heaven's sake, if there is a chance you might catch something edible, go to Tupper. We took our lightest fly rods to the stillwater above Buttermilk Falls, caught a pail full of minnows, and left for Tupper.

On the road out of Long Lake village we picked up a one-legged hitch hiker. We had supposed he was a tramp, but he said he was a lumberjack looking for work. He had been turned down at Finch Pruyn headquarters near Newcomb yesterday and now was on his way to Tupper Lake Junction to hop a train to the next lumbering town. Winters he worked in West Virginia, preferably in the timber, but sometimes in the mines. It was there he lost the leg, falling under a car in the mine yards. Each summer he comes north seeking work, and it is harder to find every year. Last summer he found nothing, although he tried everywhere in New York, New England, and as far east as Millnocket in Maine. Here it was the first of August—he said it looked as though he would be out of luck again. Formerly he could always find a job in the north and work until snow began to fly.

I asked, "What do you do? Cook?"

He said, "No, if I did I'd have to board out myself."

This was no ordinary man. He had a strong, interesting face, lean, with eyes set deep under slanting brows, and a long, broken nose. It was the face of an El Greco bishop or martyr of the faith. He was a very observant man. He spoke rapidly of lumbering in West Virginia, describing the forests, the terrain, naming all the lumber companies in the state and where they operated. I said again, "What do you do? Drive team?"

"No," he said. "I'm not fit for that." He never did tell us what he was fit for, and we did not prod him again.

We took him to the Junction, then drove to the mouth of Bog River where it rushes across the ledges in a charge of white water and shoulders its current a hundred yards into the wide lake.

Bop took the ledge on the east side of the stream; I crossed on the bridge to the west. We drifted our live minnows down the rushing water. Soon Bop had a bass and I caught a walleyed pike. Bop got a walleye and hooked into a second bass. Ed had gone up to the bluff to cook lunch, I was on the ledge across the current, and Bop had to net the fish himself. His feet went out from under him and he slid down the steep rock on his back into three feet of water. His first pass with the net from a sitting position, water to his neck, missed, but the hook held. Another pass and he came dripping from the water with a three-pounder thrashing in the net.

73

On the ledges at the mouth of Bog River.

The sun was bright and hot after the rain, and the dip he said was pleasant. Over the island in the distance was a haze. I retreated to the shrubbery seeking shade, meanwhile watching the rod, propped over a stick and held between stones. It began to shake, the prop collapsed, rod and reel went scraping down the ledge. I raced after it and grabbed the handle at water's edge. In came my second walleye.

"That will teach you not to go doping off in the shade," said Ed. "You darn near lost a rod."

"Doggone, I'd like to catch a bass," said I. "My side of the current has nothing in it but walleyes."

"We came to get walleyes," said Bop. "You take this side, if you prefer, and I'll cross over."

Sport is the thing the bass fisherman has in mind; food is the consideration in catching walleyes. I am not knocking the pike-perch as a stubborn game fish or the smallmouth bass from Tupper and other rocky Adirondack lakes as table fare. They are in fact right palatable if not dried out in cooking—far more so than the bass of weedy ponds. But we had been eating bass all summer and there were twelve people at the camp demanding a change of diet. I suppose there is no disagreement among gourmets that next to whitefish and lake trout, and of course brookies eaten the same day they are killed, the pike-perch is the best of freshwater fish to eat.

My minnow had barely reached the lake when it began running sideways off the current and I had a strong fish on the line. It did not leap, but I knew I had a fine bass—it was so strong, and of course the bass were all on this side of the current. Then I got it in close and saw another walleye. I reached to net it at the edge of the water and my feet began to slide on the slippery rock exactly as Bop's had done. I fought to get my balance and to keep from falling backward on the granite, so I toppled forward and flopped on my belly in the lake. I came up without the fish, too, and the laughs were on me, even though I had wrenched an ankle and was limping.

"Your turn, Ed," I said. "Here, take the rod."

"Not me," said Ed. "It's more fun to watch."

From across the current, Bop was catching walleyes and bass too, which did not help.

Late in the afternoon a man and his girl came to the bank above us. Love was strong in them and they did not care who saw them. They lay in ardent embrace until Bop hooked a bass that ran back and forth and leaped high several times. Then they sat up and watched the fishing until we left with our catch. The man said they would have to try the fishing sometime. We said no time like the present. They split themselves laughing at the tremendous joke and we laughed along with them. Overhead was a bright blue sky, but cumulous clouds were building rapidly on the horizon. From the distance came intermittent rumbles of thunder.

At the Sources of the Hudson

ORIGINALLY there was no fish life in the waters above the high falls of the Opalescent. Trout were carried to the Flowed Land sometime in the 1840s or 50s and from there introduced to Lake Colden, Avalanche Pond, and Livingston Pond. In the 1930s, when I often fished there, Colden and the Flowed Land were full of beautiful squaretails. Trout of one to one and a half pounds were common; we occasionally caught one of two to three, and Clint West, the state's resident ranger, had taken them to four and a half. As these fish were nourished only on insects and crustaceans—with of course such smaller trout as they were able to catch, but no minnows or coarse fish—they were beautifully colored, deep bodied, and delicate in flavor— the most delicious trout I have eaten anywhere.

The waters were ideal for fly fishing. They were nowhere very deep and at 2,750 feet remained cool throughout the summer. Even in mid-August the trout could usually be interested in surface food. One did not have to look for spring holes; the Flowed Land was all one big spring hole. The same for the smaller ponds and Lake Colden, lying between the granite flanks of Mt. Colden and Mt. McIntyre.

In Colden the fishing was often best along the dark line that marked the movement of water from Cold Brook, perhaps because of the supply of oxygen it was bringing in, plus the fly life and the hatches which developed at the mouth of the brook and were then carried out on the current and the winds, but it was not always so. We spent a lot of time on that brook channel when we could more profitably have been working the weed beds.

Although the fly fishing in Colden and the Flowed Land was as good as you could find in the eastern United States at that time, anglers would occasionally lug a pail of minnows up the steep trail from Lake Sanford, hoping to entice the trout with a live succulent offering of the real McCoy. Clint West, however, knew that he had something unique and precious to guard in these waters that held no other fish but trout. Too many Adirondack ponds had suffered and some ruined by the introduction of bait fish, including God only knows what predacious trash. It was in this decade, in all probability, that the first small fingerlings of yellow perch were liberated in Cranberry, eventually to multiply into the swarms that resulted in its destruction as a trout lake. It is the habit of thoughtless fishermen to dump their unused bait minnows in the lake at the end of a day's fishing, perhaps as a goodwill offering to the trout. Minnows can also escape from a bait pail hung over the side of a boat. Clint took no chances and ruled that all minnows had to be dumped on the grass and killed before they could be taken in the boat. I doubt that Clint's Law was ever violated, for he had the quiet confident air of authority that men naturally respect. Besides, he controlled the boats.

Clint himself often wished for a mess of bullheads. Trout were all right, but bullheads satisfied a deeper hunger.

On his way back from Minerva, where he visited his family and picked up supplies every ten days or so, he would stop at Lake Sanford and catch bullheads for his supper. In his first years at Colden he was sometimes tempted to bring them back alive and release them from his dock where they could multiply and provide him with a ready change of diet. He decided to think about it before acting, fortunately, and came to realize that the presence of the bullheads could only degrade both the quality of the trout and of the fly fishing. Once he had made the sacrifice he was more vigilant than ever in seeing that no one brought live bait to Colden or the Flowed Land, and he began prodding the fish and game people to nail the matter down by restricting the waters to fly fishing only.

The trout of Avalanche and Livingston ponds were numerous but small. Clint had a special interest in Livingston, which lay only three hundred yards from the Flowed Land. He saw Livingston as a nursery for the Flowed Land, supplying it from its own abundance in periods of high water. Anglers who fished Livingston were instructed to limit their catches to what they intended to eat that day. Fish and Game at Albany were asked to ban the use of bait and lures on Livingston, at least.

No action was taken on Clint's recommendations that I know of, perhaps for the reason that fishing pressure was so light on the back country ponds in those years. The fishing of the high Colden valley was not well or widely known, and some who did know of it preferred more accessible waters. The trail to the Flowed Land was rough and steep, five or six up-and-down miles from Lake Sanford, a three-hour hike with supplies on your back. Unless you also carried a boat, you might have to fish from a raft or the shore when you got there. The State kept one flat-

Clint West, ranger at Lake Colden, a man ahead of his time. In the 1930s he campaigned unsuccessfully to have the lakes restricted to fly fishing only. Regulations to this effect have since been adopted by many states for their blue-ribbon trout waters. *Photo courtesy of* The Conservationist.

bottomed rowboat on Lake Colden and one on the Flowed Land, both for use of the ranger. You could borrow a boat from Clint if he was not about to use it, or if it was not being held for his return from wherever he might be working that day. If one boat should be free, but two fishing parties happened to be present, the boat time had to be shared between them, half a day for each. Clint would change his work schedule to oblige a fisherman when he could, but that was not always possible. He had much to do. There were miles of trail to keep brushed out, and seven or eight lean-tos to look after, one of them at Lake Tear-of-the-Clouds. These he kept supplied with fresh balsam, wall to wall, and stacks of firewood, including the kindling, neatly piled and ready. Life held no greater pleasure than to arrive at a Flowed Lands lean-to and fall into the deep, springy balsam, nothing more required to make camp than to roll out the sleeping bags and put the pan of butter in the spring.

After our first trip we solved the boat problem by carrying up a cedar guideboat and leaving it with Clint. It would be ours to use whenever we came to Colden, and Clint's the rest of the year. This freed the work boats for other fishermen on days we were not there.

The waters were little fished, water temperatures were always near perfection, and usually our luck was good. If we did not tie into fish on Lake Colden, we found them on the Flowed Land and vice versa. Once in a while they would not move for us, particularly in cold, windy weather, and during the first week of August 1936, there were five such days in a row. Fishing ten or more hours a day, two

81

men casting, one rowing, we would take a fish or two in the morning, and perhaps the same or nothing at all in the afternoon. One morning I left the boat, climbed Mt. Colden, and lay there in a hollow among the summit rocks, lazy as the puffball clouds that drifted across the face of McIntyre, supremely indifferent to whatever the frustrations in the tiny boat below. Bop turned to worms that he found in Clint's garden and got fish enough for a chowder from the one deep hole in the lake. Then late in the afternoon of our last day the wind died, the air mellowed, and I began picking up fish on the dark Montreal. I had been kidded unmercifully since morning for sticking to the fly while Bop was proving as he had the day before that the trout would take a worm. Fishermen learn to endure this gaff.

Ed: "I thought we came up here to catch fish."

Bop: "You and I did."

Ed: "What did he come for?"

Bop: "You tell me. Maybe to improve his casting."

Ed: "But what good does it do him? He can't catch a thing."

Bop: "That's what you call a purist."

Ed: "I heard of them. They're better than we are."

Bop: "True, they're more sensitive."

Ed: "Would they eat a trout caught on a worm, or are they too pure for that?"

Bop: "They rationalize it some way. The one I know will consume but not contribute."

Ed: "We ought to rationalize him. The grub is getting low."

We were drifting around in the middle of the lake most of this time, so I was not being given an equal chance, as I pointed out. More hilarity. Equal chance became the theme.

82

Bop: "How many worms did we use up yesterday?"

Ed: "Two dozen, maybe more."

Bop: "We caught ten fish. We fed fourteen that went free."

Ed: "That's what I call equal chance."

Bop: "The court should cite him for contempt of trout."

Ed: "That's going pretty far, though, seems to me."

Bop: "Are you trying to defend him?"

Ed: "Not exactly. Just trying to figure it out."

Bop: "Did you know he uses minnows on occasion?"

Ed: "Hell, he uses them on bass and pike all the time."

Bop: "Frogs, crawfish, even nightcrawlers."

Ed: "Nightcrawlers! How sneaky can you get?"

Bop: "If it's all right for bass and pike, why isn't it for trout?"

Ed: "He has more respect for bass. He thinks trout are pretty stupid."

Bop: "He's finding out today."

They split themselves laughing. I had to grin and bear it.

The sun was down behind Mt. McIntyre and the valley in deep shadow when we left Colden for our lean-to on the Flowed Lands. Perhaps we should have gone sooner, for although the lakes were close together, fishing in one often was first rate when the other lake seemed dead. We were hungry and Ed was rowing fast as we went down Opalescent Brook. Bop had taken in his line, but I kept casting ahead to every likely spot. I raised a half-pounder off the big rock in the brook, which was encouraging. Then as we entered the lake proper I hooked into three fish, one after another. The first came off the point of a boggy reef.

83

It was the best fish we had taken all week by far. The second was a very much bigger fish, perhaps the biggest squaretail trout I have ever had on the line. It came from midway of the same reef and made a stirring picture, leaving a wake behind it as it sped toward the fly and striking it in a turn that formed an imposing whorl. For a moment I felt the power and solid weight of a big one. Then he was gone with the fly and part of the leader, leaving that swirl behind for all to see. There was silence in the boat as we drifted slowly on toward a fallen balsam top, and I replaced the leader and fly. The first cast to the tree brought a splash and I was tied into another good fish. Bop reached for the net again but Ed said, "I'll handle it; you get a fly on the line." A few minutes later, from the other side of the fallen balsam, Bop got his fish.

The three fish we took in that brief flurry weighed over four pounds. The eleven we brought from Colden, most of them caught on the worm, weighed but three.

"They're just beginning to hit," said Ed as we sat about the fire. "We should have come up next week, dammit. I wish we could hit this place just once when they were really rising."

"We've done well here in the past," said Bop.

"But I mean *really* rising. All of them, all the time rising."

Ed's wish to see a spectacular rise on Colden was to be granted, but we missed fishing it. We went up one Thursday in July of 1936 for a single day. In those years getting fish for Friday dinner was the most important duty

84

Near the foot of Lake Colden, looking toward Avalanche Pass. Mt. Colden is on the right. *Photo by S. R. Stoddard. Adirondack Museum, Blue Mountain Lake, New York.*

of the week. Fish for Friday we must have, and since the kitchen could not depend on our bringing in a catch on Friday, Thursday's fishing was equally critical. It sounds like a joke, but we rarely had luck when fish were most wanted at the camp. Fortunately Mr. Lahey kept a shelf full of canned salmon at his store in Long Lake, and there was an old pensioner in the village who could supply us with bullheads, skinned and dressed, for 35 cents a pound. Three Fridays out of four we ate salmon loaf or bullheads.

On this Thursday Ed Wallace and I hit the trail to Colden, arriving at noon. The lake was perfectly still. From half-way across we could see the ring of a solitary fish feeding off the western shore. Other fish broke the surface from time to time in other parts of the lake, but there was no sustained activity anywhere. By following up the scattered rises, however, we had our requirement of nine fish by five o'clock. Mission accomplished. We were almost three hours from the car; it was time to start back. We put in at Clint's dock to clean and pack the fish, and took down the rods. We crossed Colden, left the guide-boat at the outlet for Clint, and took the trail down Opalescent Brook to the Flowed Lands. Clint was in the work boat at the landing there, trying for a big fish that he had lost the day before. We watched him for a few minutes. Ed discovered that he was missing one joint of his rod; we had left it behind on the bench at Clint's dock. "I'll rush back and get it," he said. "I'll row faster with only myself in the boat; you visit with Clint."

Twenty minutes later Ed came running down the path, excited and breathless. Fish were breaking shore to shore on Colden, he said; we just had to go back there. I shook my head. "Then we'll be going down Calamity trail in the dark, and we said we would never do that again." We had done it in September the year before. I had fallen crossing Calamity Brook, soaking myself to the neck, and we had almost set the woods on fire with the birchbark flares that we lit to see the trail. Clint was still giving us hell for that, although we had been careful to stamp out every spark.

Ed said, "Man, you've got to see it, at least. There's more fish breaking out there than we see all summer."

Clint said we could spend the night at his cabin. He would make us comfortable and be glad of the company. I said we had promised to be back soon after dark. Clint said we could phone from the cabin and explain, hit the trail at daybreak, and be back in camp by nine o'clock in the morning.

I have always been slow to change my plans if it meant disappointing other people. This is weakness in a fisherman, but it helps to keep the peace. If we had not already caught our Friday fish, I would of course have turned back. This was the over-riding priority. But we had the fish, a rare accomplishment, and there were three women with the children alone at camp. They were self-reliant women and safer in camp than they would have been at home in the city, but still. The place might catch on fire. Someone might break a leg. My sense of responsibility was strong, now that we had our fish. We said goodbye to Clint and shoved off.

A month or so later we were back at Colden for our annual week. Fishing was excellent, we had some big ones keeping cool in the spring, and were feeling smug. We visited with Clint one night and heard some yarns of the days when he had been a guide at the Tahawus Club. I asked him what was the best day's fishing he had ever had. He said it had been on Clear Pond near Long Lake, fifteen or twenty years before. "I could have filled the boat with lakers that day if I had wanted to. Seemed every time I let the spoon down there was another fish waiting for it."

I said, "But I meant what was your best fishing for squaretails with the fly." He thought it over.

87

"We used to have lots of good fishing on Preston Ponds years ago. Here too. But—well I have to say that the very best was one evening here this summer, right here on Colden. It was earlier, maybe four, five weeks ago. I was rowing across the lake. Fish were breaking everywhere, but I didn't stop to cast until I saw the size of some of them that were cruising on the surface. The air was full of the little smoky wing flies with brown bodies, and the trout were zig-zagging after them, left and right, tails and back-fins and sometimes their snouts, too, out of water. I made exactly four casts out there with the old Queen and caught four fish, and I had to come in and weigh them. I knew I had more than ten pounds of fish in the boat and I was right. I had more than twelve. One of them went four and a half."

"Just when did you say that was?" asked Ed.

"Back in July. Come to think about it, it was the last time you were here. It was the same day I was up at Lake Tear. Sure. I was talking with you fellows at the Flowed Lands just before I came back to this lake."

The best fishing of a lifetime. Ed and I stared at each other. He grinned. "Don't look so glum, Vincent," he said. "You had all the fishing you wanted, remember?"

Colden—Alt. 4712

ALGONQUIN CONFRONTS IT across the narrow valley in which lie the three little lakes—Avalanche, Colden, Flowed Land, and the little pond, Calamity. I had seen it from Algonquin's top, across the gulf in which the white birds maneuver far below, clear and sharp against the sky, an outline created by the earthquake and landslide of several centuries ago. This sheared it down, clearing it of humps and terraces, so that on the western side it is one sweep of naked rock, from top to bottom, at an angle which seems to fall back little from the perpendicular.

A sign on the nearest highway, fifteen or so miles away, announces its altitude as 4,712 feet. Other mountains are about it, but it seems to lift itself apart from them, a flying summit, shaped rather like a triangular sail with the top squared off.

I had seen it from Calamity Pond meadow with sunlight flooding the pink and gray granite of its western wall. And I had seen it at night more than once from the little foot bridge where Flowed Land sluices into Calamity Brook. After stumbling through the spruces for half an hour, in darkness so thick that the man behind could not see the man ahead even when he bumped into him, Ed Wallace and I would sit resting on the bridge before going on, and look up at the mountain, softly lustrous in a night full of stars.

Then one morning I woke up in a lean-to on the Flowed Land. There was the mountain as usual, the fishing had been slow for three days, and there could be no better time to climb it.

It was a bright morning, blue and cool. I sat on a log by the fire, and in view of the job ahead of me, ate a pound of beans. I had not eaten a pound of beans for breakfast since I was seventeen. But this morning I felt the old bean hunger, and when bacon, eggs, pancakes, toast, and the salmon-fleshed trout of Flowed Land on top of orange juice and blueberries failed to remove it, I ate the beans. Then I cut a staff of tamarack, which is a light wood but tough when it has not been weathering too long, and shook hands with Bop and Ed as though we were parting for a long time.

The first part of the trail follows the Opalescent and you can walk it in five minutes. But this morning I seemed unable to move freely. I had to remember to put one foot ahead of the other. My muscles were tight and cramped from twelve hours in a boat the day before; I was still sleepy; I was too full of beans. All this kept me at a very deliberate pace. I began to think of Goldsmith's Traveller since I felt exactly like him: *"Remote, unfriended, melancholy, slow—"*

Dr. Johnson told of a man who asked Goldsmith what he meant by "slow." Did he mean "tardiness of locomotion?" Goldsmith said he did, but Johnson disagreed. "No sir," he said, "you do not mean tardiness of locomotion;

you mean that sluggishness of mind which comes upon a man in solitude."

Given the context, I had thought when I read it that Johnson was right, but now that I was having some experience of it myself I saw that Goldsmith knew what he meant, and that while the sluggish mind might be implied, he was thinking of a sluggish body, too, and probably in the first place.

The Opalescent above the Flowed Land is a swirling brook, twenty to forty feet wide, eight or ten feet deep near the lake, twelve inches deep a quarter-mile above it, very clear and cold. Where Lake Colden trickles into it over a shallow dam, it bends away at a right angle, and here I had to ford it, for my trail went up along the shore of the lake. The going became rougher, up and down over the rock ledges. One rock stands up twenty feet above the water; there I sat and rested. Across the lake Clint West was carrying wood to his cabin; soon the smoke began to rise from his chimney against the dark green wall that goes piling up toward the bare, lofty crown of Algonquin. I had been up there once, on a day when I was fit and hungry, and I would get up Colden, too, before the day was done. Meanwhile, no cause to hurry.

At a point opposite the ranger's cabin the trail turns away from the lake and climbs up through a mixed stand of hardwood and cedar, including some of the grandest cedars left in the Adirondack forest, toward the outline ridges at the side of the mountain. It is possible to go up the rock face, taking to the trees only here and there, but much easier to make this flanking movement along the trail. Roundabout as it is, you will yet mount 1,962 feet above the lake in a hike of something less than two miles, roughly a foot in altitude every five feet of the way.

To the left of the trail is a deep ravine, bedded with moss-covered hunks of rock, among which the outflow of a spring falls in a continuous twisting line of white water.

A wind came curling in from the direction of Avalanche Pass. I began to feel livelier, forgot all about the Traveller, and went up at a good pace for twenty minutes, still following along the edge of the ravine, until it shallowed out and ended in a damp wall of rock. I had a drink here from the top source of the spring, crossed along the rock, and went on up. The grade became stiffer, and shortly I observed that the hardwoods had about disappeared; a hundred feet above that, the evergreens grew densely together and began to dwindle in height. Where the trees were no higher than my head, I came upon a pile of immense rocks which have fallen together so as to form a covered alleyway through which the trail goes.

I emerged from the rocks on a back ridge of the mountain. Now the flanking movement was completed and there was no more easy going. I went up and over the ledge on a ladder that Clint West built one day, not so much for the convenience of Travellers as for his own. This brought me into a field of laurel, several acres of it, all in bloom. It was a dwarf growth, but the flowers were large and massed densely together like flowers in an exhibition garden. What made it more astonishing was that this was August 1, and the laurel of the Appalachian valleys had bloomed in June.

Above the laurel is a hill of rock and above that the level and narrow summit. I went toward it, feeling the elation that comes to everyone on mountain tops, and nowhere else that I know of. It comes I suppose from the release of your eyes to great distances, from your immersion in air and light, and also no doubt from the sense of accomplishment, at having for once gotten somewhere, in fact to the very top.

I sat looking down on the lakes, tracing the weed beds and shoals in Colden by the patches of darker and lighter water. Flowed Land was shaped like a snapping turtle with its head stuck out; if the men who named it had seen it first from here they might well have called it Turtle Pond. Clint West wants to rename it even now; his choice is Lake Opalescent, after the brook. I can see reason for renaming a lake that bears the name of some forgotten notable who did not discover it, never lived beside it, never knew it existed until it was proposed to name it after him, but to change the beautiful, distinctive name of Flowed Land would be a move in the wrong direction.

Above and beyond the lakes were the familiar mountains looking unfamiliar—Santanoni, looking from here like the broken edge of a saw, from the Cold River valley like a sleeping animal, cat, or panther, and like a ruined castle from the Newcomb side; Adams, and all the others piling up in long ridges one behind the other to the horizon, like the waves of a stormy sea.

I had been looking toward the west. Over the northern shoulder of Algonquin is a valley with meadows, green and yellow, laid down amid the forest. Now the shadows of clouds began to drift slowly across that country, all the way to a sizeable lake, with a spire or two standing up beside it, which I thought must be Placid.

The wind changed; the clouds came drifting back along the humps of Algonquin and, catching some updraft of air from the lakes, rose and sailed off down the gorge of the lower Opalescent, their shadows following them.

Suddenly I turned, for something had caught my eye. There to the east stood a pleasant-looking hill with rock-encrusted slopes, and for a moment, because it was so near and plain, I did not know it. It was Lot 49, Township 45, of the Totten and Crossfield Purchase. It was the

93

peak of Marcy. This noble mountain is also known as Tahawus, the Cloud-Splitter, though generally referred to by the name bestowed on it in 1837, in honor of William Learned Marcy, then serving his third consecutive term as governor. New York has had many governors since, enough to have renamed all the mountains in the park, if it had been proposed and if the public had put up with it. Some of them have been at least as eminent as Mr. Marcy. There was Mr. Al Smith with five terms, Mr. Tom Dewey with four, and Mr. Nelson Rockefeller, also with four. And there were the two Roosevelts, each with only one term, but see what happened to them later. None of them sought to re-christen Santanoni or Haystack in his honor. The time has come to restore to the highest mountain in New York State the beautiful Indian name, Tahawus. Here is a name change that every son of the Adirondacks, native and adopted, *in situ* and *absentia,* would welcome.

Now that I saw it so close I resolved to climb it, some other morning when the sky was blue and bright. Then I knocked my pipe on the topmost rock of Colden and went down to learn how our fishermen were doing. Turned out that in my absence they had had good luck; in fact they had caught fish enough for supper and breakfast too. True they had done it by forsaking the fly and fishing with worms in the deep holes of the lake. But while Clint West has been crusading to have the waters reserved for fly fishing only, and on his own authority forbids the use of live minnows at any time, he does not turn his back on starving men who must catch their trout on worms. In fact he himself had shown Bop and Ed where to dig. Everything considered it was easy to forgive them their escapade. A pound of beans will not hold a man forever.

The Last Day of the Season

THE MORNING WAS DARK, still black as night when I woke up at twenty minutes of eight, so that I could not believe the clock until I heard the clattering of dishes and voices in the kitchen below. When I got downstairs Ed Wallace came in and said, "Well how about it? It's pretty late for Colden now and it's going to rain like hell. But how about it?"

I said, "Call up Clint and ask how it looks up there, and we'll decide after breakfast."

"Clint says they're not hitting. There's a party of five men in there and they haven't caught a fish in four days. He said he would bring the boat to Flowed Lands if we want, but he thinks it's not much use. Looks like rain up there, too."

I said that I did not care about the party of five, but had Clint caught any?

"He would have said so if he had, so he hasn't. What about it? What do you think?"

I thought it would be tough to go up there in a cloudburst and not get a damn thing.

"That's it," said Ed. "Tell you what. We could run down beyond the county line and fish one of the streams,

Fishing Brook or that Vanderwhacker Brook, there's good fishing in there, or how about the Boreas River?"

I said we should think about it at breakfast.

"Yeah," said Ed, "better get some food. Food brings counsel."

So we sat down to breakfast. The windows were open wide and the air seemed marvellously fresh, soft, and humid. Any rain would be a warm one, and though the sky was like night, I had a conviction it would be strange if we could not catch trout on a day like this. It had been cold and blustery for a week, but yesterday had been bright and warm, there ought to be some insect life astir now, and a warm moist day like this should bring it out. So I said let's go, and Ed called Clint.

We stopped on the way to try out Fishing Brook, which was a waste of time, and it was ten o'clock when we reached Tahawus post office and stopped to get Mike Breen's permission to park on the grounds of the Tahawus Club. Mike was superintendent there. If we could park at the Club and go up Calamity Brook trail we could be at the Flowed Lands by twelve-thirty. If we had to go by way of Lake Sanford and the Opalescent River it would take at least another hour. Mrs. Breen was at the house but not Mike. She had no idea where he was or when he would be back. If we sat around waiting for him we might still be there at noon. I had a hunch we would run into Mike if we got going so we drove up the Club road looking for a blue Buick and saw it coming our way. It pulled up beside us and Mike Breen said, "What the hell you doing on this road? You've got no damn business here! Who in *hell* you *think* you *are*?"

His face and voice were so angry I thought he had not recognized us in the car, so I jumped out. "Mrs. Breen said . . ."

"You get straight the hell out of here! You go on the Club property and the two of you'll be chewing daisy roots."

I said, "Well, Mr. Breen, we are only trying to find you. It's the last day of the season and . . ."

The grin came immediately when he saw that he had me buffaloed.

"Why sure," he said, "you go ahead. Gee I wish I was back there. Haven't any paper and pencil with me, and they'll try to stop you. I ought to be there. Tell you what," he roared again, "You tell 'em Mike Breen said to park your goddam car by the barns and they can call me up at the postoffice if they don't like it, and I'll tell them what to do."

There was of course no problem. We were stopped, but the message, considerably modified, was accepted. Mike Breen at the time was the tyrant of the Tahawus Club, much esteemed and endured by the club membership whom he professed to disdain. The Club kept a considerable herd of Jerseys that often got out of the pasture and gave Mike no end of trouble. It seemed a large herd for the membership. Two-thirds of it could be got rid of, said Mike, "but the sons of bitches drink nothing but cream."

By ten-thirty we were parked and on the trail. The air was heavy. We were hot and soaked at the first crossing of Calamity Brook and stopped to rest. Ed said it would rain like hell any minute. I wished it would hurry. Half an hour's rain and lightning ought to clear the air.

We took five again at the top of the Big Heap. Suddenly we felt much stronger. The climbing was all behind us and we hit a faster pace. I said I had just this minute got my second wind, but Ed said didn't I notice it was cooler now and the air lifting?

Rain caught us at Calamity Pond meadow and held

97

us in the lean-to there for half an hour while we ate our sandwiches and drank our beer.

"Be hell if we had to spend our last day here listening to the rain," I said.

"We'll get a break soon," said Ed. "Raining too hard to last."

It was after one o'clock when we arrived at the Flowed Lands. The water was calm and the color of lead. A rowboat and a raft were on the lake, two fishermen in the boat, one on the raft. Clouds hid Mt. Colden but were parting along the flanks of McIntyre. Avalanche Pass was visible between the clouds.

Our guideboat was at the landing where Clint had left it. We rowed slowly along the ledges that rise on one side of the Flowed Lands, casting as we went along, then past the boggy land beyond the ledges and into the mouth of Opalescent Brook. Girls were swimming and shouting in the big rock hole which is usually good for a fish, and Ed said, "College Week is here. Damn, I'd hate to be spending a week here with all this clatter."

"Wait until you look the girls over."

"Hell," he said. "Let's go on up to Colden."

We slid up the outlet of that lovely sheet of water between the two big mountains, and I felt the elation I always do at first sight of it. I said it was great and I didn't mind the whooping. Ed grinned. He said it's great even if you don't catch a fish.

"But we've got to catch fish on a day like this. I could smell fish on the air all morning. I know we'll catch fish today."

"Well, let's go out and catch four. That would be about right, eh?"

"Plenty."

We cast along the shoreline and then worked the mouth of Cold Brook carefully before landing to talk to Clint. He asked if we had raised anything. We said not a damn thing.

"I raised a good one in the Flowed Lands this morning bringing up the guide-boat and lost him. I had an old leader that had been drying on the rod and it cracked at the hook. But that's the first fish I've seen in a week."

"Anything at all been breaking?"

"No, not a sign of fish."

Ed checked his watch with Clint's clock. It was two-thirty. I said we'd better get moving. There's not much of this fishing season left.

We worked Cold Brook again and then the logs and ledges on the eastern shore with no result. I took off the black bucktail and tried other flies, finally a grey ghost which looked wonderful in the inky water. Finally we moved over to the weed beds off the mouth of McIntyre Brook.

"Now," said Ed, "put on a little fly and go to it."

"All right," I said. "I think I've got a Van Patten here."

He dug his oar into the mud. "If you don't get one here we may as well quit, eh? Good God I'm sleepy."

He closed his eyes and hung on to the oar. I covered the hole halfway out with no luck. A bubble broke on the water beyond casting distance, and I heard a little spat. It came again, in the same place.

"Dammit," said Ed. "We haven't seen a sign of a fish stirring. Goddam funny we don't see a break."

"There's one dimpling now on the other side of this hole but I can't reach him just yet. He's right over there."

I pulled off more line and cast it in the general

direction of the bubble. A fish took hard and I said, "Here's the first one." It was a twelve-inch fish, chunky, small headed, highly colored like all the Colden trout.

"Doggone," said Ed. "Now we only need three more like him."

"Move me to the right about twenty feet and a little nearer the weed."

He did and as the boat began to move a fish swirled within ten feet of us. I dragged my fly through the swirl and missed a strike. I waited and cast back. We plainly saw two fish dash at the fly, but I raised the rod too quickly for the short distance and pulled it away from them.

"Be damned, we were right in the middle of them," said Ed. "When we come back, we'd better anchor farther out."

I heard the little spat again and now we were near enough to reach it. On the second cast I hooked the mate to the first trout.

Ed said, "There's two of them. Now if we can pick up one by the brook maybe we can come back here and get the odd one eh? One of those you missed."

We rowed into the mouth of McIntyre Brook and tried the logs where in the past we had raised so many small trout that ordinarily we shunned the place. But today nothing. Once again we worked down the long channel of Cold Brook that is Clint West's favorite spot and probably ours, too, since we keep gravitating to it. We landed and talked to Clint, who was playing horseshoes with one of the college crowd. He said, "You've done pretty good. I didn't think you'd do a darn thing."

I said, "Haven't you got a good one hidden out some place? We'll go get him."

100

Ed said, "They'll hit all right if we can find them. But by god they seem to be scattered all over in this cold water."

Clint said our best chance would be off the mouth of Cold Brook or off McIntyre. But we said we had tried them both.

"Then up toward Avalanche," he said. "Should be fish in the mouth of Avalanche this time of year."

We decided to hold Avalanche in reserve, a place to try when the weed beds needed resting. We knew there were fish in the weed beds and they had been rested now the better part of an hour.

"It's not so discouraging now," said Ed, "we only need two more. Gee, if we could only get a big one, eh?"

I said maybe we would.

"Have you got a hunch?"

"Yes, we're going to get a good one. At least a pound and a half. Maybe two of them."

We worked over the shoals toward our old hole in the weed beds and anchored there. I had not been casting long when there was a good swirl around the fly. We rested the spot, but when I cast back to it, nothing happened. A second cast, right on target. Still nothing. Probably the fish had been foraging and now had gone to cover. I pulled out more line and shot it well over the spot to the edge of the weed. A fish struck heavily and held there.

I said, "Well I've got him, and he's a good one."

Ed said, "Yay, goddam it, we'll get our four fish yet."

The fish came toward the boat, then swung away and his back fin showed briefly. Ed said, "Well, he *is* a good one."

101

The trout made a long run parallel to the weed bed. I wondered why it did not run for the weed and found out when it stopped, the line began to lift under the strain and the tip of a branch rose above the water.

I said, "He's hung me. Let's go."

Ed pulled up the oar and we drifted toward the snag, which turned out to be a waterlogged bush, complete with root system. I caught hold of it but could not unwrap the line with one hand holding the rod.

Ed said, "Pass it down here. I'll break it off." I dropped the bush, keeping the line taut. Ed got the line free and pulled the old bush into the boat. He was a little excited now. "Can't lose this one. By god, look out, he's running for the weeds."

But the weeds did him more harm than good, and after we had coaxed him back into deep water he was about through. He zipped back and forth and under the boat, then began to roll, and I steadied him into the net.

Ed said, "There, by god, the whole trip's paid for."

Up at Clint's landing, two hundred yards away, we heard voices. Somebody was saying, "Those fellows in the guide-boat just caught one." It should have been a warning that competition might be expected here if we did not hold our place, but we were not alert to that. It was time to rest the hole again, and we moved away to fish the mouth of Avalanche Brook. There is a wonderful deep hole here, a Currier and Ives picture of a hole, with big rocks in the background and two large trees tumbled in the water for cover. Once again we learned that the trout were not where they should have been. We worked here for half an hour. Only our flies disturbed the calm. When we got back to the lake another boat was anchored at our spot in the weed bed. We fished up the shore to Cold Brook and for the

102

fourth time worked the channel of the brook before landing at Clint's dock.

Ed said, "Well Clint, will he go three pounds?"

"Just about," said Clint, "What did you get him on, the old Van?"

"Yes, we got all three on it," I said. "We tried other fiies but that's the only one that took fish."

"Sure," said Clint, "because it's a good fly. That's why I kept looking for it so many years. But those we had years ago were bigger, number eights and sixes. Seemed like the fish took them better."

"Doggone it," said Ed. "We wanted four fish, but the only place they'll hit is that weed bed, and it's taken."

"Don't hog it," said Clint. "There's always next year."

We said good bye and rowed away. The clouds and mist that filled Avalanche Pass were shot with light. In the sky above us was one small patch of blue. From far down the lake resounded the whoop and holler of sixty college boys and girls. Ed shivered.

"What's the matter, Ed?"

"Look at those damn fools in swimming."

Ed carried to the Flowed Lands. At Opalescent lean-to a dozen of the college crowd were making fires, drinking coffee, standing around. There was excitement as Ed went by with a boat on his head. I followed with the trout. A lad who seemed to know about squaretail fishing leaned over. "Boy, oh boy, oh boy!"

A slip of a girl with little pink cheeks and golden hair looked with interest at my hat and my heart began to ache.

"Now there's something New Hampshire ought to have," she said.

103

"My hat? Or the flies?"

"The button. We have licenses in New Hampshire but we must carry them in our pockets."

Ed said at the landing, "Must I hogtie you to get you home?"

I said "There's a time for everything, I hear, and trout season is over."

We went across Flowed Lands leisurely, fishing the creek outlet, fallen tree tops, ledges. A fisherman at the ledges called, "How many?"

"Three."

"On a fly?"

"Yeah."

"That's some encouragement. I haven't raised one in four days." But he would keep on, he said. Last year at nine-thirty on the last night of the season, he got a two-pounder.

At six-fifteen we left the boat; thirty minutes later we were at the top crossing of Calamity Brook. It was dark now, but for once we had thought to bring a flashlight. There was a brief alarm of rain on the leaves overhead; then it came sheeting down. We pulled on our rain jackets and plodded along. Sliding down the Big Heap we heard shouts of joy and welcome below. Two hikers, drenched to the skin, came stumbling up the trail. They were on the way back to Colden, saw our light, and thought we were friends coming to find them. They had left the gang on Lake Colden at noon, hiked down the Opalescent to the old strip mine at Lake Sanford, then to the head of Lake Henderson before turning back to the outlet and the Calamity Brook trail. Ed figured that at the point we met them they had already covered about fifteen miles. They were dog tired and had been having trouble in the darkness and rain keeping to the trail. They rested with us five minutes, slumped on a log in the rain. It was now seven-thirty and they had a good three miles ahead of them. Ed advised them to go slow and wait for their friends or daylight at the lean-to in Calamity meadows. The trail from there on would be narrower and impossible to find without a light, should they lose it.

At eight-fifteen we came to our car by the barns of the Tahawus Club, and ten minutes later we were in Mike Breen's kitchen, having an old-fashioned with him to cap the season and the day.

Post Season: A Day on Algonquin

W E GOT OFF to a bad start, the day we went up the
Algonquin Peak of the McIntyre mountains. First the
weather looked uncertain, and we held off, waiting for it to
clear. Then when we had parked the car in a patch of brush
beside a sandy road, a red-headed woman appeared and told
us to remove it beyond the confines and boundaries of the
club's property, which meant driving it back about a mile and
a half. Ed said we were not aware of our trespass. He said he
had parked here when carrying fish up, for the state, in
the spring.

"You're not carrying fish now," said the lady. "A
little walk won't hurt you."

This was mid-September 1934, before a letter from
Father George Boucher, of Long Lake, had opened the way
for us through the club's formidable caretaker, Mr. Mike
Breen.

Ed appointed himself to take the car back, being
younger and in better shape, as he reminded us. Chuck and
I went ahead, carrying the knapsack. We passed the club
buildings, crossed Calamity Brook, and sat down on a log to

McIntyre Mountains as seen from the west shore of Lake Colden. *Photo by S. R. Stoddard. Adirondack Museum, Blue Mountain Lake, New York.*

wait for Ed. We had about seven miles left to the peak. The trail forked here, and a sign pointed left to Indian Pass, 6.1 miles, right to Lake Colden, 4.5.

Soon Ed came along. We saw him a hundred yards away, as he came out of the bush and on to the gravel patch beside the brook. He was almost running. We stood up and called as he splashed into the water, and he grinned at us, not because he was happy. He was sweating and out of breath. He peeled off his shirt and wiped his forehead with it, and then reached up to hang it on the sign.

"Disagreeable woman," he said. "She was sitting on the porch, watching the road and she said 'Now isn't that much better? Don't you feel much better leaving your car where it belongs instead of on other people's property?' "

"What did you say, Ed?"

"Why argue? I tipped my cap."

He dug for a sandwich in the knapsack. "Better eat, you birds. Not going to stop again until we're on the peak. Judas! We won't be there by night, at this rate."

So Chuck and I each ate a sandwich, too. There was steak in the pack to be cooked later on, and a grouse that Ed had skillfully run over as we were driving up.

Ed drank in the brook and said, "Let's go." We reminded him of his shirt, hanging on the sign. "No," he said. "Leave it there." We said he was being foolish. It would be cold and windy on the mountain. We might run into rain up there.

"No," he said. "To hell with it. I won't be bothered," and walked ahead. Chuck rolled the shirt up tightly and stuffed it in his pocket.

We were then at the foot of the Big Heap, and for the next half hour we were too short of breath to waste it talking. The Big Heap is made up of five little heaps, with short level spaces between them. At the top of the Heap, the trail again crosses the brook. We came out of the dusky forest into the sunshine, and knelt on the slanted rocks to dip our hands in the stream and splash the ice cold water over our faces and the backs of our necks.

Here it seemed to us that the air had taken on a different quality. It was thinner—it had the feel of height in it. Down below us was the long sun-filled alley of the gorge.

Over the tops of the trees we could see no higher ground. We felt that we had reached the rim of the world.

But we had a way to go yet. Half an hour farther on, we came again out of the trees, this time to cross an old beaver meadow, and from its edge we had our first sight of Mount Colden. It rises up from the lake like a great pink battle axe in the sky, one of the most spectacular mountains in the East.

On the far side of the beaver meadow, a little apart from the alders and the tall wild grasses, is a monument of some soft Italian stone, a honey-colored pedestal cemented whitely to a rock beside Calamity Brook. It has been there for more than a hundred years now, in the memory of a man who lost his life on that rock, and whose name was David Henderson.

We stopped for a moment, and rested in the dry autumn grass, and Ed told us the story of how, in the year 1846, David Henderson and his small son were traveling up the brook in the company of a guide named John Cheney.

We rose and went on, Ed walking first, then Chuck, and myself in the rear. The trail was steep here and rough, with sudden turns among sharp rocks, and our breath came short. As I listened to Edward speaking of the fame and good renown of John Cheney, I realized that there was a cadence in his speech, and that his words came like the words of a poem.

He was a very famous guide, he killed so many moose and deer
    and panther,
everybody thought he must be Leatherstocking, or the other
    way around;

He worked for this Henderson, and Henderson must have
    thought well of him,

109

I believe it was him named that pond Lake Cheney for John.
No doubt he knew his way through the woods and was a pleasant
    companion,
yet I judge he was a careless, absent minded man and a danger-
    ous man to have around with a gun.
You know there was once he shot himself in the ankle—
He was paddling after a deer, and his gun was beside him in
    the canoe
and cocked and his foot near the muzzle
God Almighty, he was lucky he didn't blow it off.

Then on this trip I've been telling about, he borrowed a pistol
    from Henderson,
and after a while gave it back to him cocked, by Judas!—gave
    it back cocked!

And never said nothing about it, so later on
when Henderson took off his belt, the pistol went off and
    shot him,
and he lay down there on that rock, and as he lay dying,
Cheney came up, and Henderson did not abuse him,
only he said, "You left the gun cocked, John!"

And ever since then they've called it Calamity Brook,
although farther down of course they call it the Hudson River.

That was Ed on the subject of John Cheney, as we
went on and up through the birch and hemlock forest, and
crossed the head of Calamity Brook where the lake called
Flowed Lands comes piling out through an old sluice.
The best going was now behind us. From Flowed
Lands to Lake Colden it is about a mile over a narrow up-
and-down trail. The footing here is not very good, for the
only soil is what the crowding trees have made for them-

Headwaters of the Opalescent, on its bed of feldspar and granite. This view was probably of its junction with outlet brook from Lake Colden. *Photo by S. R. Stoddard. Adirondack Museum, Blue Mountain Lake, New York.*

selves, gradually filling with fallen needles the crevices and wells between the jumbled rocks. So in wet weather the going is soft, and in dry weather it is slippery, and in either case you whack your skins and ankles against the rocks unless you go very slowly and with care.

We tried to make time, and stumbled left and right.

Now we could hear running water below us, and soon we saw rocks and a deep brook slipping between them.

111

It was the Opalescent, coming down off Marcy to the Flowed Lands. Here we stopped to breathe, and as we looked down into the long glen below us, we saw a fox coming along the river side beneath the wind fallen trees. A very large and beautiful orange fox he was, his four black legs swiftly moving among the ferns. He passed below without seeing us, relaxed and easy in his own domain.

"Heading for town," said Ed. "Nothing in particular on his mind."

"What is it, Ed, a cross fox?"

"Of course not. What made you think it was a cross fox?"

"Black legs."

"All foxes have black legs," said Ed, "Didn't you ever look at one before?"

"They look different alive," said Chuck. "Bigger and more beautiful."

"It's the truth they do," said Ed. "And that was a very fine young fox."

At two o'clock we walked into the clearing which surrounds the ranger's cabin on Lake Colden. Through a gap in the trees we could see floating in the high sky like a cloud, the round and rolling head of the Algonquin peak. It looked a very long way up there. It was not three miles, but it looked like ten.

Ed was beginning to fret. We had made slow time in. He supposed we would be three hours more getting to the top. Chuck and I said we could make it in two. Ed looked doubtful.

"Maybe we could," he said, "if you had gone to bed a little earlier. Or if you could keep from talking the rest of the way." He pointed to my basketball shoes, which always

112

annoyed him. "Or if you weren't wearing those dam tennis slippers."

Half a mile past the ranger's cabin we came to a brook and to a fork in the trail. The path to the right went on to Avalanche Pass, and then down into the South Meadow country. The left went up along the brook to the Algonquin.

It is a very handsome brook, tumbling steeply into narrow box-cut basins as bare and clean as porcelain. These basins are all in the lower course of the brook near the lake; higher up it is all one long twisting series of white cascades, broken only in one place, and there by a long ramp or flume, where the brook comes smoothly down a slanting face of rock. The water comes down the left side of the rock; we went up on the right.

After that we had a stretch where we could climb, as if up a ladder, along the exposed and tangled roots of trees.

"This is where Heffernan gave out," said Ed. We knew that story of the year before, when Ed had gone up the mountain in fifty-five minutes, leaving three of his friends stretched out and gasping like fish on the trail behind him.

We went on and up. "One nice thing about this climb," said Ed. "No dips in it. You don't have to climb everything twice."

Chuck turned round and grinned at me. We were too shortwinded to speak.

Then the mountain leveled off for a spell, and in an hour from the forks we came to a place where the brook split around a big flat rock. Ed said this was a halfway mark, and he wanted to eat. Chuck and I washed our wrists and faces, and stretched out on the rocks. We thought it would be better to eat after we had climbed the mountain.

Ed let that pass, because we were soft, and he was not. He broke out the cigarettes, and we sat up to smoke. Through the thinning tops of the trees, we saw birds wheeling out in the gulf between us and Mount Colden, and in the narrow valley below was a far line of lakes and brooks flashing between them.

And behind Mount Colden now we saw for the first time the overtopping pyramid head of Marcy.

Ed wound up a story about bears. He had thought of bears because these mountains, Colden and McIntyre, are their favorite wintering places. There are many good holes to den up in, and no trappers.

We stood up again, ready to go. Ed lifted the knapsack and put it down again. He said, "We've carried this far enough. There won't be any wood or water up there, anyway. If you guys won't eat now, you'll have to wait until we come back down."

There were three or four pounds of steak, a loaf of bread, a grouse, and a small flask of whiskey in the sack. He hid it in a hole beneath a rock and blocked up the entrance with logs, throwing them around until they were tangled like a windfall.

The mountain got no easier. We stopped a lot to breathe. Just before reaching the spruce line, Ed stopped and pointed, and we looked up to see the high crown of the mountain, a great worn hill of rock, lavender, and olive, formidably above us in the shining air. Below it and to the right was a long drop, beneath an overhang.

"That's the way we'll go up some other day," said Edward, "if you ever get in shape."

The spruce line is very straightly marked, as though it had been run by a surveyor. This is the point at which hardwood trees must stop, and above which only the spruce

114

can grow. The spruce trees at the line are twelve or fourteen feet in height. As you go on up the mountain they dwindle rapidly and evenly in size. Soon they are no higher than your knees, and then you walk out of them altogether into sloping acres of moss and low creeping shrubs.

It was four o'clock. We walked on easily now, and to the right, the left, and behind us, the ground all fell away. The air was very clear. You would have known from the quality of the air and light alone that you were on the mountain.

We found some dew pools and drank from them. They tasted no worse than river water, or not much. We saw patches of a white flowering moss. A small bird hustled among the shrubs. Ed said that deer would not climb so high.

Now we came among boulders the size of houses. From the top of one of them we looked down into Avalanche Pass and the valley beyond it, all painted with the bright smoky Indian colors of the early fall. The scarlet of course was maple, the yellow was maple and birch, the burgundy, ash, and the buckskin browns and copper were the great stands of beech. Folded into the hollows of the mountains were green patches of pine, cedar, spruce, and balsam.

Ed was getting restless and probably a little chilly. He watched the sky. There were a few white clouds which seemed high up and distant, but now a small one drew toward Mount Marcy and settled there, clinging to the peak.

"I'll go down now and get supper started," said Ed.

"Wait a minute," said Chuck. "You can have your shirt now," and pulled it out of his pocket. Ed grabbed it and grinned.

"Chuck," he said, "I love you."

115

Chuck and I stretched out in the sun and smoked. We got down to the spruce line at a little after six o'clock, and before we got there we could smell the smell of toasting bread and broiling steak. We came hustling down.

The meat was burned crisp on the surface but full of juice inside. We ate it in a hurry. Ed was worried. Colden and Marcy, in full view of us, were still in sunlight, but the shadow of Algonquin was already over the lake below, and over the valley through which we would have to travel home. It would be pitch dark down there in an hour or less, said Ed. "And it's almost ten miles to the car. Let's get going."

We went down the mountain in a hurry, running when we could. At seven-thirty Lake Colden was behind us, and we were on the narrow trail to Flowed Lands. It was so dark in there that you could not see the trees, even when you bumped into them. And the resinous green spruce and cedar pressed us so closely that we did not dare light a torch.

The mile of trail between the lakes took us almost an hour. We slipped and fell. We stubbed our toes and shins at every step. I was now walking in the middle, Ed ahead and Chuck behind. Chuck said thank God that I was wearing my white basketball shoes, because they were a guide for him in the darkness. "Damn tennis slippers," said Ed.

Then we came to the log bridge at the head of Calamity Brook. In the little clearing there we had the light of the stars to see by, and it made a big difference. From here on we would have a four-foot trail, most of it through the tall hardwood, and it would be safe to light torches, even in this dry weather.

We found birchbark in the clearing, folded it, and stuck it into the clefts of two green hardwood sticks. We lit one and Chuck held it while Ed and I looked for more birch trees, and stripped enough of the loose bark to fill the knapsack and our pockets. Then we set out, Ed in the lead and making new torches on the way, Chuck in the middle carrying the light, and myself in the rear, stamping out the sparks. There were lots of sparks and they fell far and wide, so that I zigzagged home like the mailman walking back and forth across the street.

Up ahead I heard Ed telling Chuck the story of the deer he had wounded with a rifle shot and tried to finish off with his knife, only to have it carry him down the hill two hundred yards, slamming him against trees, and cutting his sheepskin to ribbons with its hooves.

For every step they took, I was now taking three. I could keep up with them only because they had to stop so often to light another torch. The flares threw a long flame, trailing black smoke as though they had been soaked in kerosene. Some burned for only a minute, some for three or four minutes. Stiff bark gave the best light and burned the longest.

Ed told the story of the big fight when Bob Glasbrook held off seven men until they doused him with a pot of boiling water.

After what seemed a long time, we came to the brook crossing at the top of the Big Heap. Now for the moment we lit two flares, and by their light we crossed the stones without wetting our feet. This made us so confident that Ed tripped on a root and fell sideways into the bush, and I dropped through a rotten piece of corduroy clear to my knee. That made us more careful, and we got down the rest of the Big Heap without a bruise. After we hit the wider trail below, I seemed to go asleep, and next day when I set down my notes I could remember very little of this last stage. I have one separate memory of the three of us around

117

a big paper birch, stripping down loose sheafs of bark, and when we had taken all we could reach, Ed went up it like a bear, clawing it as high as the first branches.

Then I remember as we came on to the loose gravel near another crossing of Calamity Brook, where the trail goes through a deep, narrow gully, the birchbark flare seemed to burn more brightly and give a more lurid light. The dark figures of Chuck and Ed ahead of me stood out more clearly, and I could see the glint of water just ahead. Ed balanced himself on the crossing log and then stepped down.

"We'd better wade this one," he said, and we did. The water was not quite knee deep. It was cold and felt good on our tired legs and feet. Part way across I stumbled and fell in.

"There's one in every party," said Ed.

Once again, a long time after that, I seemed to have been dozing and for a moment came awake. I remember thinking that the brook crossings were behind us and becoming aware that we were out of the woods. The flares had been discarded; there was starlight enough to see by on the wide road we now had. Chuck and I were walking side by side. Ed was a step ahead, his white shirted shoulders swinging easily. But he must have been tired too, for he was not saying anything at all.

The Adirondack Days
of Henry Abbott

MR. HENRY ABBOTT, his old friends used to say, had found the fabulous fountain of youth that Ponce de Leon could not find in Florida. Abbott found it in the Adirondacks, probably in that spring hidden on the back slopes of Mount Kempshall that he wrote and talked about so much. It was even rumored that he took jugs of it back to New York City where he attended to a watchmaking business when he was not off camping in the mountains with his guide Bige Smith of Deerland. The acres of ginseng he found growing in the shade on Santanoni, roots of which he brought back to prove the story, could have had something to do with it, too, if the Chinese were right about ginseng. There might well have been a grain of truth in it, for he looked a good twenty years younger than his eighty-one when I first met him in July of 1931.

Largely out of consideration for Bige, whose legs and feet were beginning to feel the discomforts of arthritis, they no longer made the extended rambles through the forest that he described in the tales he wrote for distribution at Christmas to his friends. But every day of the summer, Sundays excepted, was still spent at a camp and hideout on

119

the west shore of South Pond—the Rowan-Wood of one of Mr. Abbott's tales. The two-and-a-half mile hike over the golf course hills and through the woods to the outlet cove where they kept a varnished guideboat, its oars suspended on wire and pulley from the trees where the porkys could not get at them, was just an hour's easy breather. Visitors like ourselves usually drove to a landing on the east shore opposite the camp and paddled or rowed ourselves across. It was not in the spirit of Rowan Wood, but it was permitted, we being merely fishermen and guests.

Mr. Abbott was a fisherman, too, but at this time his main interest was in what he called "pioneering." He enjoyed building with logs, using no other tools than the pioneer might have had—axe, saw, and hammer. In the years before the state banned the construction of permanent camps in the forest preserve, he and Bige had built six widely separated cabins as bases from which to push deeper into the woods. Now over the course of several summers they built on South Pond a cabin with twelve windows, a lean-to where they slept in fine weather, a boat house for three boats, a dock with a rock crib to protect it from the ice, a wide stairway of split logs laid into the steep bank above the shore, a dining pavilion near the head of the stairway, roofed and floored but open on all sides to the weather and the birds, and close to it an outdoor kitchen, similarly open, with a fireplace.

Pioneering also included the repair and improvement of all this, brushing out around the cabin yard, cutting wood to replenish the perfectly arranged wood pile, hiking over the ridge to the burnt land on Pine Brook to pick berries, and transplanting rare ferns and wildflowers to the cabin yard. Four long-stemmed orchids rising eighteen inches high from two large, broad, polished leaves at ground

One of the wild orchids transplanted by Henry Abbott and Bige Smith to their South Pond Camp, Rowan-Wood.

level, were their particular pride. Mr. Abbott said the plant was uncommon in the Adirondacks, and these had been found one by one in widely separated places.

Fishing, of course, had its place. When the morning was overcast and calm, with that fishy feel to the air that every experienced fisherman can sense, Mr. Abbott would cast his flies over the spring hole in the outlet cove and then to likely lies along the shore as Bige moved the boat slowly and cannily along. Or Mrs. Abbott might have ordered a whitefish for dinner, in which case they would tie up at a buoy where Bige would have scattered a few quarts of cut bait the evening before. Usually they got the whitefish, with once in a while a square-tail trout or two, and once a twelve-pound laker, the occasion for one of Mr. Abbott's amusing yarns, even more amusing when retold at lunch one day, with details and embellishments he had neglected or suppressed when writing about it.

Lunch when guests were present invariably meant potatoes baked in the coals of a wood fire and a thick steak grilled above. Charcoal was held in abomination because of its noxious fumes and association with backyard cookery. Birch, hard maple, and beech, with cedar for kindling—nothing else was permitted. Mr. Abbott, who had invented the stem wind-stem set arrangement that revolutionized the watchmaking industry, the calculagraph that still today times and records our long-distance telephone calls, and altogether fifty devices concerned with the measurement of time, of course had determined to the second how long Bige was to grill a two-inch steak. A gold-cased Howard watch was open beside him on the table, and he sat with his eyes fixed upon it, ready to say "Turn . . ." and "Done!" After 1933, Canadian ale cooled in the spring was there for those who wanted it, and always a pot of coffee made fresh as needed with water bubbling in the traditional lard pail hanging from a hook above the fire.

Many a post-lunch hour, while a summer breeze stirred among the pines, ruffled the surface of the pond, and died away, Ed Wallace and I sat there fascinated as Mr. Abbott and his friend James A. Emery told their stories. Mr. Emery's were of the west where he had grown up, of Maine and the Laurentians where he had fished and hunted in his early middle years before acquiring Pine Point Camp; Mr. Abbott's were of the things he had seen and the men he had known in more than forty Adirondack summers.

122

Bige Smith had his own fund of tales when we could get him going, which was not always. He resented the coming of age which kept him out of the back woods and made him keep to the house in winter. He was always more cheerful and talkative in July when Mr. Abbott was back at the lodge and summer was ahead of them. By September there would be long silences. If he spoke at all then it was only to answer a question or to grumble that he could not enjoy summer for thinking how soon it would be over. Once he said he would like to be God Almighty long enough to change the landscape around. He was tired of seeing Owl's Head in the same old place on the left, Blue Mountain always standing to the right, and "I and Abbott can't go look at 'em from the back side any more."

Mr. Abbott had no quarrel with age, if he thought of it at all. He once refused to give his age to an interviewer on the ground that it was not pertinent to the interview. "You will find it on my tombstone," he said. "Until then it has no relevance." He had been coming to the Adirondacks since about 1880, at first on ten-day fishing and hunting trips, later, after a serious break in health, to spend the three months of the summer and in some years the fall as well. His was the typical case of an Adirondack cure, as dramatic as any the historian Donaldson has described. Carried up to Deerlands on a stretcher, not expected to last the month, he was on his feet in a few weeks and six months later felt well enough to return to town. "It taught me to spend as much time as possible in the out of doors," he said. "And since that was my inclination anyway, I did not resist."

This happened in 1890, when he was forty. Thereafter he and Bige lived the life that many have dreamed about but few realized. "The best times of all were in the

123

1890s and up to about 1914," he said, "before we had gasoline boats on Long Lake, and the roads did not encourage
long journeys by auto." Then full summers were passed
without meeting another camper, and they moved as they
pleased through an Arcadian setting in which the animals
of the forest watched them with more curiosity than fear.
On a dark night in July, Bige would kick the burning logs
together and the shower of sparks would be reflected in the
shining eyes watching from the darkness. Bige would lower
his voice and choose his words with care so that his audience
would not take offense or suspect him of nature faking.
Fishing and hunting, which at first had seemed an end in
themselves, later became "mere incidents" to fill an empty
larder, while the charm of "wandering with senses alert" to
the forest presences increased with every visit.

Leaving Deerland at sunrise, they often rowed and
paddled the fourteen-mile length of Long Lake, plus several
miles more down the outlet water and up Cold River,
portaging around its rapids as necessary for a ramble of two
weeks or more on Seward and Santanoni mountains. Once,
leaving the guideboat on Cold River, they hiked back and
forth all afternoon along the flanks of Seward, Bige carrying fifty-two pounds and Mr. Abbott thirty-seven, looking
for the Lost Pond that might not exist at all except in the
uncertain memories of the oldest woodsmen, for it was not
marked on the map, and no man living could tell them
where it lay. They found it at dusk, a sheet of water clear as
air over a white sand bottom, and on its shores a curious
log covered with moss six inches deep. Peeling the moss
they found beneath it a dugout canoe that had been carved
from a pine log generations before, but with some patching
was still usable. Dark was coming on, but they postponed
supper for twenty minutes of the greatest fishing Mr. Abbott

Henry Abbott and Bige Smith, brother of boatbuilder George Smith, starting out for Lost Pond, circa 1902.

was ever to have, the most exciting, and for the strongest, most vividly colored trout. They ate supper by firelight and decided that with such fishing to be had, their planned stay of three days should be stretched to four. Turned out they had to leave the wonderful place next morning, however, when porcupines ransacked their packs and destroyed all their supplies. Home was almost fourteen hours away and they had their breakfast at nine o'clock that night in the kitchen of the lodge at Deerland.

Another time, with full pack baskets and a tent, they set out from South Pond, which is in the watershed of the

St. Lawrence, and climbed the ridges easterly until they reached the summit of Fishing Brook Mountain and went down its northern slope to find and drink from the topmost spring of Fishing Brook. Studying the topographic maps, Mr. Abbott had decided that this was the true source of the Hudson River, for it was the most remote from the sea, and in both length and volume of water it was greater than the eastern stem which bears the name of Hudson where the two meet at the outlet of Harris Lake.

One of the cabins they built in those years was at the southeast foot of Mount Kempshall, where they found the large spring boiling out of fissures in the rock. The brook that flowed from it was not deep enough for fish of any kind, so with logs and rocks they dammed it in five places to create five pools, and stocked it with small trout caught on barbless hooks in Pickwacket Brook two miles away. The trout survived and multiplied and several years later perhaps the greatest attraction at Camp Hatchery was its brook where schools of fry could be seen darting through the shallows at any time of day, and adult wild trout swirled and leaped in the pools at evening.

They came to know and recognize individuals among the animals and birds, a buck with a looped antler tine first seen when it peered through the open door of the tent where they were sleeping, a golden eagle that ranged the valley of Long Lake and Cold River from Wildcat Mountain to Santanoni, a beaver with a white patch on its head that they met again and again through seventeen successive summers, often miles away from its own house on Cherry Pond. Mr. Abbott told its story in "The Chief Engineer." Younger beavers would build and rebuild a dam that the first torrent would destroy. Then the animal with the white patch would appear, a new site would be chosen, a proper dam built, and the Chief would return to Cherry Pond. Its skill and experience were reflected in ever larger and more complex projects, one of them a dam with a central span of 120 feet and wing dams that brought the length of the barrier to 670 feet. Another was a canal, three feet wide and twenty-five hundred feet long, with thirteen dams and sluiceways to float a winter's supply of popple down to Cherry Pond.

There are photographs all through Mr. Abbott's nineteen little books, bound in simulated birchbark covers, that tell of these observations. We see the two men starting out with their packs to find Lost Pond, Abbott slight and spare, age about forty-eight, dressed in Norfolk jacket, knickers, white shirt and bow tie, and Bige in his overalls, a large man, round faced, looking the five years younger that he was, although in time to come it would be Mr. Abbott who appeared to be the younger man. We see Bige on a platform that they built high aboveground between trees, from which they could watch the animals of the forest unobserved. One of the mysteries that woodsmen talk about is how beaver can keep their winter supply of the light, buoyant popple wood submerged at the bottom of the pond without the weight of rocks to hold it there. Bige had his theory and we have a photograph showing him trying to suck the air from one end of a popple stick while the other is immersed. It did not work, but only because he did not have a strong enough sucker, said Bige. We see Mr. Abbott (dressed as usual in the manner approved by Hardy Bros. Ltd.) returning to camp with a grouse he had shot for supper, and in another scene, minus the tie and jacket now, but still in white shirt, he teams with Bige to pull a saw through a log they had felled near the South Pond cabin. We learn from the text that the log was almost three feet

127

Henry Abbott returning to the tent with a grouse for supper.

through at the stump, and that they cut and split twenty-four blocks from it in one day. The pile of firewood that resulted appears to have been arranged with a carpenter's level and plumb lines. It so impressed a male grouse that he tried it as a drumming platform.

The precise lines of the woodpile were typical of Mr. Abbott. A good watchmaker is a perfectionist by nature, and this can be exasperating at times to those about him. Bige would groan when Mr. Abbott emerged from the Deerland cottage carrying his large camera and tripod to announce that they would make pictures of birchbark for the next Christmas book. "What's wrong with last year's picture?" he would ask, well knowing what the answer would be. Mr. Abbott wanted a different picture each year, if possible a better one, but anyway different. "I'm not repeating last year's story. A new story should have a new picture on the cover." Off they would go, Bige toting the camera equipment and the makings for lunch wherever they might find themselves at noon. Sometimes they had the pictures by that time, and could lunch at Rowan Wood, but not always, for it was not any birch tree they came upon that satisfied Abbott's idea of what he needed for the new cover. A considerable tract of forest must be traversed systematically, back and forth in parallel marches like a drill sergeant inspecting the troops at rehearsal for a dress parade, critically examining every detail, missing nothing. When a tree was singled out by Abbott, Bige would cut out a generous slice of bark, Abbott nervously watching, bidding him don't cut too deep now, might wound the sapwood. A photograph would be made and they would go on to another tree. Mr. Abbott must have a number of samples, all carefully chosen, to select from. Back home, Bige would have the family in stitches as he pantomimed Abbott scrutinizing a birch. "Him use last year's picture? You don't know Abbott. We got to spend another day like a couple of woodpeckers hopping from one tree to another and getting crosseyed with our noses going up and down against the bark."

Many of the stories we heard at South Pond were never put on paper. When I suggested he do so he said, "They are about people instead of animals and I don't feel at liberty to write about them." One of which I made a note in my journal concerned Dr. Le Boutellier—"Le Boot," Mr. Abbott called him—a New York physician who, like

129

Abbott, first came to the mountains on brief holidays to hunt and fish. Le Boot bought land on Long Lake, not far from the Deerland Lodge, and another tract on South Pond, extending from Mr. Abbott's line to the outlet. He preferred the place on South Pond as being removed from the village and highway, and there he planned to build a year-round home whenever the lady he had in mind would marry him. But after years of promises and stalling, saying she was needed at home to take care of her old parents and so on, of course she married another. Le Boot left New York City for good then and built his house on the pond, a fine Victorian mansion, turreted and balconied, overlooking the outlet cove. He was hoping that his mother and sister would come to live with him. They did in fact try it for a few summer months, but departed with the chill airs of October, and Le Boot was left alone in the big house, a Thoreauvian retreat with amenities. He had himself appointed health officer of the township without salary, and began a long campaign to raise the local standards of health and sanitation. "He had expected to be received as a benefactor in this township that had no other doctor, and to be listened to with the same respect as the preacher," said Mr. Abbott. "But now that he lived here he was just another neighbor and that's all his advice was worth. So the cloud of flies around certain kitchen doors and milksheds was thick as ever, and they never could believe it was important to get treatment until they were flat on their backs. No one could be so weak minded as to run to the doctor for a cough, for example—result was he never got to treat a cold but he saw plenty of pneumonia. To get their respect he began to charge the same fees he used to receive in New York, and when I teased him about it, said 'It will teach them to listen to me. If they would take care of themselves, they'd not be sick.' Actually it made no difference; nobody paid him anyway."

Through the winters Le Boot wrote long letters to Mr. Abbott. He did not like to see the changes that the automobile was bringing in. He would write that in other years the winters in Long Lake had been full of excitement, with sleigh rides on the lake, tobogganing on the hills, square dances on Saturday night. "But the automobiles cannot travel in twenty-four inches of snow, so now there are no dances or parties, but we sit at home and quarrel. . . . No one has been sick lately but Mrs. Jones. She was badly off for a time, and we thought she was a goner. The village cleared the road of snow from her door to the cemetery, anxious that Plumley's new hearse should not be stalled in a drift or slide off into a ditch. Mrs. Jones heard about it and got so mad she recovered in a day. I am happy to report that the new hearse is as yet unused."

Mr. Abbott said that for all his grumbling, Le Boot was a sentimental man, with a strong attachment to the people of the mountain villages. He preferred the company of craftsmen like George Smith and guides like Bige and Leslie Palmer, the silent, the aloof, to that of most of the summer people.

"He had a hope that when his time came to die, it would be at South Pond, with his eyes fixed on the summit of Blue Mountain. So he got my permission to cut down several of my trees that blocked the view from his bedroom window. Day or night the curtains were left open to that view. He wrote that it was a glorious experience to wake on a clear night and see the dark mass of the mountain beneath a sky filled with stars. He did not get his wish,

131

however, for in his last year he found it necessary to move to Dave Helms's house in the village when cold weather set in, and that is where he died."

Another tale that regaled us during a South Pond afternoon concerned the Long Lake steamboat line. There were several large private camps below the village that could be reached only by water. At the end of the lake was a hotel, and in that area too the summer home of Mr. Henry S. Harper of the publishing firm. Mr. Harper's guests arrived in squads with wagons of baggage. They alone could fill a steamboat several times a week. Tourists passing through the Adirondacks could be expected to board the boat for a view of the lake. On every pleasant summer's day the steamboats on Raquette and Blue Mountain Lakes carried many of these one-time passengers. "The fact that Raquette and Blue Mountain had such boats had something to do with the wish of the Long Lakers to have one too," said Mr. Abbott.

George Smith, the master guide-boat maker, was commissioned to build the steamboat. George's boat shop was at Deerland, on the upper end of the lake. He had served his apprenticeship in guide-boats at Saranac, arriving there around 1884 from Agawam, Massachusetts, where he and Bige had been raised. Chances are that he worked in the boat shop on Lake street under William Allen Martin, who was the first to build the boats with planks feathered into each other, and so light they were known as "Willy Martin's egg shells." At any rate George Smith's boats were second to none in beauty, stability, and lightness, yet so durable that many are in use today, this half-century after their maker's death and ninety years after he set up his own boat shop at Deerland. It took some persuasion to coax George Smith to give up the guide-boats for a year

A guideboat built by George Smith. The Adirondack white cedar planks are $\frac{3}{16}''$ thick. Knees and stem are of local spruce, cut to follow the natural grain. Length, 13′ 9″; weight, 45 lbs.; it can easily carry three men. This boat was built some time before 1927, and it is still (1977) in daily summer use.

and turn to building a steamboat, but Mr. Harper had the gift of words and it was done. George built the boat with the help of his brother-in-law Sam Smith in time for the start of a new summer season.

An elaborate party was arranged for the first trip down the lake. Hampers of food and tubs full of ice for the champagne and beer were taken aboard. Henry Harper's guests came from far and near. There were speeches and fiddlers at the dock, and the boat steamed off to the cheers of the guides and visitors at Deerland Lodge. All went perfectly until arriving at the pontoon bridge across the narrow waist of the lake at Long Lake village. The boat could not clear the bridge. Someone noted that Cold River was in flood again, and whenever that happened, the flow of the Raquette was reversed and both rivers poured into the lake, raising it by several feet. Of course Cold River was not always in flood, but by the time summer was over it had become apparent that there would be few seasons when the water would be low enough to permit the boat to pass. Some years later the old bridge was replaced by a new cantilever structure high enough to clear an ocean going tug. But by then the gasoline launch had been introduced, to Mr. Abbott's regret, and there was no need or demand to refurbish the Deerland steamboat. By the year 1931, when I heard the tale from Mr. Abbott, the weathered hulk could still be seen lying amid the weeds above the now tumbled-in boat house that George Smith had built for it. It was a beautiful boat, with the graceful lines one might have expected of the builder. Someone said it was a pity no one had had the means or the vision to have it hauled overland to Lake Champlain or the Hudson River where it might have had a long and useful life. Mr. Abbott said it had in fact been advertised for sale, but long hauling was a much more difficult matter in those days, and only the engines found a buyer.

It was an amusing story until one saw the boat lying there. Then one could only be sorry for the builder, and the boat that had outlived him, but not in the way he had planned. George Smith died in the 1920s. He was working underneath a large gasoline launch one day when a chain slipped, the boat came down, and he was crushed beneath it. People said George had never had any luck with power boats.

"Back there around the turn of the century," said Mr. Abbott one day, "Mr. Henry Harper owned most of the land at the foot of the lake and tracts of forest on either side. With or without a steamboat, the Moynihan Hotel promised to be a nuisance, so Harper bought it, tossing in a section of land around Anthony Ponds as part of the deal, and transformed it into a guest house. I often visited there, on my way to or from the Cold River country, and ate in a dining room that had once been a bowling alley, eighty feet long and twenty feet high. One spring the caretakers, cleaning up in preparation for the summer, stuffed a lot of rubbish into a fake fireplace and touched it off. The place burned to the ground and was never rebuilt. Harper himself about that time had lost his enthusiasm for the Adirondacks, perhaps as a result of the death of his first wife. She had loved the woods and particularly this neck of it, miles away from the village and road. His second wife was a much younger woman, who apparently had no interest whatever in spending her summers in the backwoods. I suppose they might have reached an accommodation, if he had wanted it.

But perhaps the mountains had never really taken hold of him, as they had the first Mrs. Harper."

Bige, who was hard of hearing, had been following the story by catching a word or two and knowing the rest by having heard it all before. "Dang fool, if you ask me," he said.

Mr. Abbott gently smiled. "He was really a nice fellow. But new friends, new interests, they say."

Mr. Abbott himself was probably the best story of all and another time he told us a good part of it. We heard how he arrived in New York in the year 1871, age then twenty-one, to set up his own watchmaking shop on Maiden Lane. Watches of the day were as thick as your thumb, several inches in diameter, and weighed a quarter of a pound. Advanced models were set with a stem and wound with a key, but they were still thick, large, and heavy. They were usually carried in the pocket of the vest and anchored with a heavy gold chain, looped through a buttonhole, and terminating in the opposite pocket. "The farther west you went, the heavier was the chain," said Abbott, "and when I went to San Francisco, I thought I understood why so many men were round shouldered."

He had come to New York with an idea, which was to wind the watch with the same stem by which it was set, and do away with the key. Once this was accomplished, you might go on to make watches that were thinner and lighter and would let a man stand erect. By the time he was twenty-two he had perfected the device, and began converting the watches of his customers, at least those who appreciated the latest, into stem wind–stem set. A few years later he sold the patent to the Elgin and Waltham companies, who had been battling each other in the courts over the rights to a similar but more cumbersome arrangement, for $12,000. This sum he had fixed after the most careful reckoning and checking it over with Mrs. Abbott through all one evening and most of the night.

"You know, a Connecticut Yankee is brought up to be very particular about these matters," he said, "and once he makes up his mind to stick to it through thick and thin." Next day he was to have lunch at the old Astor House with Mr. Robbins of the Waltham Company who had been authorized to negotiate the deal on behalf of both companies. "Now Mr. Abbott," said this imposing gentleman, "you and I are about to enjoy a menu that I planned and ordered yesterday to honor a milestone in the history of watchmaking. It will also be our opportunity to get to know each other better. If you care to honor me with your views on the state of the nation, I shall be interested to hear them and to reciprocate. Our conversation can take whatever turn it will, with one exception. So long as we are at table, let's not have a word or thought of business. It's not compatible with this pleasant setting, and furthermore no aid to the digestion. Champagne is what agrees with both, however. Here it comes now, Perrier-Jouet, 1865, a flower of a wine. I have my own supply set aside here in the cellar."

Mr. Abbott went on guard. There followed blue points on the half shell, smoked Nova Scotia salmon reverentially presented and sliced paper thin, lobster stew laid down in cream and laced with sherry, galantine de volaille, roast beef, plover under glass, cherry tarts, and cheeses and the wines to go with all this from his personal stock. Mr. Abbott watched with amazement and Yankee wariness as

137

the parade of courses continued, each greeted with enthusiasm by his host and quickly dispatched, he himself meanwhile sipping a glass of champagne to be polite, but barely tasting the other wines, eating the blue points, the lobster stew, and the roast beef and toying with the rest. "I must say Mr. Robbins had an impressive way with food—and with people, too, for that matter—so with every course I reminded myself not to be swayed. Whatever he might say about it, it *was* a business lunch, and I knew it. He was not going to soften me up, if I could help it."

Two hours passed before Mr. Robbins arose and proceeded, somehow under his own power, to the lobby and up one flight of stairs to his commodious corner suite. "Now we can get down to it," thought Mr. Abbott, but no. First must come brandy and a cigar, a tour of the windows to admire the views, and a fatherly soliloquy. "What I would give to be your age again, Abbott, with your enthusiasm and drive, and this wonderful city here spread out before me ready to yield us what we would. Age has consolations, I admit, but what are they compared to the zest, the sense every moment of being alive, the strength, the confidence, the elations of our twenties? Power and prestige, my boy? Disease and mirage. Money? A puff in the wind—"

Mr. Abbott felt a choking sensation and coughed. "Smoking bother you, Abbott? Sit down, try the brandy. And perhaps it is time we talked business. We have a contract here in this desk waiting on your signature. Now you're Yankee born, I know you have given thought to the value of your patent. So tell me, what price do you put on it? What have you determined to exact from us?"

Mr. Abbott came right out with it. "Twelve thousand dollars."

Robbins reflected for a moment, nodded, and said he could see Mr. Abbott had his mind made up. But on such an occasion, there should be no haggling. "We will meet your figure. Now if you will read the document, and sign it—"

Sixty years later, telling us this story on the shores of South Pond, Mr. Abbott said, "When that had been done, he hauled from his coat a fat wallet with a wad of bills that would literally have choked a horse, riffled twelve from the top, put them in an envelope and gave it to me. He did not try to hide the wad at all, and it looked to me just as big when those twelve bills came off the top as it did before."

"To that point, I had not known there were one-thousand dollar bills in the world. The man was looking at me, however, as if to see how I would take it, and it would not do to show surprise, or even less chagrin. So I put the envelope in my breast pocket without looking into it, and said as manfully as I could, "Now that that is done, would you mind telling me, purely as a matter of curiosity, how much you were prepared to pay?"

"Twelve thousand dollars," said Robbins. "And I will add, for your peace of mind, Abbott, once the deal is made and agreed to, never fret about it. It might have gone one way as well as another."

"Well, as you can imagine, I was an unhappy young fellow when I left the hotel. I had been paid my price, yes. In those days it was enough to buy the house we wanted in East Orange, enlarge the shop, and have something left to put away. Still it was a pot of porridge when I might have made myself a rich man. But I had not gone a block down the street before I decided to take the man's advice. I said to myself, 'Henry Abbott, it was an expensive lesson, but

139

an important one, so of course it came high. Now you must apply it to good advantage.' I decided that never again would I sell an important patent outright, and I never have. Some have been leased, and when I came up with the calculagraph in 1888, I built a factory in New Jersey to make the machines myself. After all these years we are still making and selling them; in fact the market expands with the growth of the telephone systems all over the world. I have that early lesson by Robbins to thank for the fact that I did not sell the rights to A.T. & T. when they became interested in 1895."

I last saw Mr. Abbott in New York City in the spring of 1943. At the age of ninety-three, he was still spending five hours a day at his office in the Hudson Terminal Building on Church Street, commuting from his home in East Orange via the Delaware and Hudson. He had thinned considerably over the past few years, and as we left the office to walk down the hall for lunch at the Engineers Club, he asked if he might take my arm. "The doctor suggested it, and Mrs. Abbott as usual insists I follow orders." His left hand rested on my elbow with the light touch of a bird. His table was beside a window from which we had glimpses of the river whose topmost sources he had camped beside, and in another direction the lofty skyscrapers of lower Manhattan. "It was the Otis elevator that made them possible," he said. "When I first arrived here, the very tallest buildings were only five or at most six stories high because that was as high as anybody could climb."

I recalled his stories of Maiden Lane and asked when he had left there.

"Twenty-four years ago," he said. "I was no longer making watches, but spending most of my time on the

140

business of the Calculagraph Company, and it was much more convenient to be here, where my homeward ride begins." I asked which of his many inventions had given him the most satisfaction, the calculagraph or the stem wind–stem set, and heard for the first time the story of Adolphus Greely.

"If you put it that way, it was no invention at all but a bit of shop routine. In the spring of 1881 I overhauled and adjusted a watch for an army officer named Adolphus Greely. He was to make a great name for himself as Greely of the Arctic and go on to become a Major General and so forth, but at the time he was just another first lieutenant. He seemed extremely anxious that I take special pains with the job; said he must be able to rely on the watch to keep perfect time without further adjustment for at least the next two years. I had the watch for five or six weeks, checking it every morning when I reached the shop, then Greely picked it up and was off with his crew to explore new lands, reach a farthest north, and so on. It was our contribution to an international study program, in fact the first of what we have come to call the International Geophysical Years. Well, Greely accomplished all his assignments, as you probably know, but had a grim frightful time of it when the relief ships—they were commercial whalers, contracted for by the Army—could not or *did not* get through to him, so he spent the last winter, four and a half months of darkness, camped at the rendezvous point in a little hut they made of rocks and moss and canvas, everyone sick and weak from lack of food and men dying day by day.

"At least a year before this the navy had offered to organize a rescue operation. But apparently the Signal Corps felt under a cloud after the failure of their first plan and wanted the chance to redeem themselves. Probably, too, they had more confidence in the whalers—you know what these service rivalries are. But when the second attempt was a fiasco, with the press screaming and the whole country demanding action, President Arthur cut the red tape and ordered the navy to go ahead. So in the spring of 1884 the rescue ships arrived and found a handful of survivors, seven of them, all on the point of death. One did die on the way home. Rumors of cannibalism appeared in the newspapers. Some of the navy men reported that small slices of flesh had been taken from some of the dead bodies. Turned out it had been used for shrimp bait. Had there been cannibalism, the survivors would have been in better shape than they were. They were lying under their collapsed canvas too weak to raise it, and only one man able to walk when the rescue party came up. They were taken to the ships and lifted aboard at midnight in the teeth of a raging storm. You can imagine the scene on board. The navy doctors testified that Greely and five others could not have lived another twenty-four hours, and the one man able to stand not much longer.

"That fall Greely came down to see me. He wore a beard now and looked much older than the man I had seen three years before. Said he had come down especially to tell me that the watch had run perfectly through the extremities of the arctic weather and the ordeals on the ice floes; even said it was one of .the things had helped them through. Said it enabled him to plan ahead, to ration what little food they had or could scrape up, and stick to the plan. He said it was a hold on reality, too, and the fact that

142

it kept ticking away day and night through everything helped to keep his hopes up.

"Now it had only been a bit of shop work, as I said. All told I could not have spent more than an hour or two on it. But you can imagine the tingle in my scalp when I heard Greely saying that."

He took the heavy gold watch from his pocket and handed it to me. "There it is. Not Greely's, but the twin. It's over fifty years old now and still keeping time. Of course I tinker with it. Greely's could still be running too, if it has been taken care of. He used to bring it to me every couple of years or so, as long as I was in the watchmaking business."

As the story ended, I had to restrain an impulse to applaud. It had been told so quietly, reflectively, without emphasis, not rapidly but also not gropingly, with no long-winded digressions, no hesitations. The face across the table from me was not that of a very old man. It was not gaunt, there were few wrinkles, the blue eyes were alert and clear. I realized later that I had never thought of him as fearfully, perilously old, but simply as a friend I was very glad to see after an interval of several years. The only signs of age I could recall had been a certain stoop in the once-erect shoulders, the light grasp of his hand on my arm, and the lack of interest in his food.

He had begun lunch with a sip of an old-fashioned, which he said had been prescribed by the doctor, and a hot clear broth, of which he downed perhaps two-thirds. From time to time he ate a bit of a hot buttered roll, but the filet of sole and asparagus went untouched as he talked. When I said it was excellent and urged him to try it, he eventually ate half a stalk of one asparagus and took a few nibbles at the sole, no more. "I never was a big eater except in camp,"

143

he said. "But I can still do pretty well up at the lodge. There is something in that mountain air that whets the appetite."

I had not been able to visit the Adirondacks the previous summer, having entered the Navy at the outbreak of war, so of course I wanted news of Long Lake and South Pond. I had heard that Bige had died the previous autumn and asked for details. "It was sudden and unexpected," said Mr. Abbott. "He was eighty-seven—five years younger than myself, and I never thought he might go before me. We went to South Pond together for the last time only two days before I left for home, and two weeks after that he was dead. I had seen no change in him during the summer—he was still a strong man—strong enough to row us across the pond and back. Sometimes we would fish a bit at the buoy, and when I felt like casting the fly, he'd row to the spring hole in the outlet—you know that's a fair distance—take it from our dock and back. Mind you we were not making that hike across the golf course hills and through the woods —have not done that in the past six years. Oakie Helms would drive us to the landing opposite the camp—the one you generally embarked from, as I remember." He smiled and I caught the dig.

"Touché!" I said.

"Well, back to Bige. I heard some grumbling about his arthritis, but less than when he first complained about it fifteen or more years ago. Was getting used to it, I believe. He had always enjoyed plaguing me and was still at it. I made the mistake of telling him I had been knocked down by a taxicab while crossing the street. It happened out here just last spring. I got up, dusted off my clothes, told the driver to get a new set of brakes, and walked off. Bige had a lot of fun about that, any opening he saw. He

A glory that is gone, anglers on Brandy Brook Flow, Cranberry Lake. Until the mass arrival of the yellow perch, this was one of the greatest brook trout waters in the north. *Photo by Martin Pfeiffer.*

said I had more lives than a cat. Said they'd have to take me out behind Owl's Head and shoot me."

To be struck by a city cab at ninety-two years of age, brush off your clothes, and walk away without assistance must be some kind of a record. The man was amazing. After leaving him at his office—he said he had about two hours of work to attend to before starting for home— I thought I must get back to see him at least once before the summer, but I never got the chance.

145

From time to time I would hear something of him through Mr. Emery. He went up to the Adirondacks as usual in July and remained until the leaves began to turn. In early December he was honored at the annual luncheon of the Congress of American Industry, and later that month fell ill of a virus that carried him off. I have searched the index of the *New York Times* for the month of December 1943, hoping to learn what more I could of his early and middle years. The man who held that the date of his arrival on this planet was wholly a private matter—to be revealed only to his family and friends—would have been content to know that no notice whatever was taken of his passing.

Afterword

THAT KNOWLEDGEABLE latter-day Isaac Walton, the late
Ray Bergman, a long-time editor of *Outdoor Life,* philoso-
phized in his classic, *Trout,* "Somehow I feel that the elements and all life, whether human or otherwise, are directly
related—so much so that anyone who is sincerely enrap-
tured by the wonders of nature stands very close to the
Great Beyond." I don't think I have known any trout fisherman who hasn't found himself standing at one time or
another "very close to the Great Beyond"; and Vincent
Engels, the author of these tales of Adirondack fishing, is,
I suspect, no exception. Bergman began his boyhood fishing
in the Catskills, but found his fishy "Great Beyond" mainly
in the Owens River country of the High Sierras where the
"Golden" and the "Cut-throat" trout once swam, but whose
waters today speed southward through giant conduits to
those "factories in the fields" and the sinks and bathtubs of
Southern California. Mr. Engels found his in the Central
Adirondacks, gentler by far than the Sierras, but with a
magic of their own. Many of Mr. Engels' mountain waters
have also, alas, been despoiled—though by less obvious and
more sinister happenings. And thus someone like myself,

147

who remembers them before trouble came to paradise, is torn between joy and sorrow in reading this book—joy over the memories it brings back, and sorrow for those younger than myself and Mr. Engels who may never know, as we did, the full wonder of those untroubled streams and lakes some forty summers ago.

One of the things I like best about this book is the fact that the author is not one of those who go on and on about the basic trivialities of trout fishing: leader lengths, knots, "tippets," retrieving a "micky-finn," "dapping," the sinking versus the floating line, and so on. This is not a how-to book sponsored by some manufacturer of fishing tackle, but rather a heartfelt tribute to the native Adirondack trout, the once-pristine waters in which they swam, the mountains that embraced those waters, and the people— including kids with worms, "minnies," and long cane poles —who lived out their lives in those mountains and along those waters. Mr. Engels brings them all on stage in his opening chapter, "The Scene," where he evokes a haunting picture of the Adirondack landscape and its lonely fire watchers. Although some of Mr. Engel's men, including an agreeable old "hermit," may sound like "characters," I can vouch for the fact that the Adirondacks still breeds them—with the possible exception of those old-time guides (replaced today by four-wheel drive vehicles and float planes which can take you almost anywhere). The guide-boat builders' hand-crafted products, last produced on a mass scale before the 1920s, are too expensive—and can't accommodate motors.

Let me digress a moment on the subject of those Adirondack characters, since Vincent Engels seems to invite it. Not too long ago, after a day of fishless fishing on Blue Mountain Lake, trolling deep with a lead-core line for lake trout, I went ashore for a consolation drink in a local tavern. Having consoled myself several times alone with the grizzled old bartender, I thought I would try out a ballad on him which I had learned from my folk-singer friend, Frank Warner, who had learned it from an Adirondack lumberjack years ago. It was called simply "Blue Mountain Lake," and the tune was obviously an eighteenth-century Irish "Come-all-ye," written in a minor key with lots of "down derry downs" between the verses. It went, in part, like this—without the "down derrys":

Come all you good fellers wherever you be,
Come sit down a while, and a'listen to me,
For the truth I will tell ye without a mistake,
'Bout the rackets we had up at Blue Mountain Lake.

There's the Sullivan brothers, and Big Jimmy Lou,
Old Mose Gilbert and Dandy Patou—
And a good lot of fellers as ever you've seen,
And they all worked for Griffin on Township 19.

Now, one mornin' 'fore daylight, Jim Lou he got mad,
Knocked the hell out of Mitchell, and the boys was all glad;
And his wife, she stood there, and the truth I will tell—
She was tickled to death to see Mitchell catch hell!

When I had finished my somewhat off-key, a cappella rendition, my new friend grinned at me and said, "I knowed 'em all, and so did my daddy. That Big Jimmy Lou was a real brawler, and so was all the rest. They was the roughest, toughest lumberjacks in these here mountains!"

Among the other things that pleased me about this

book was the fact that the author, unlike many of my fanatical trout fishing friends in the Adirondacks, does not despise the pike, the small-mouth bass, the delectable whitefish (now largely gone in the Adirondacks) or dismiss them all as "trash fish." This ignominious term is to me the mark of the neophyte who never cast out a wriggling night crawler or a popper plug into a still pond hoping to attract anything that might be around. To be sure, as Vincent Engels points out, the pike have decimated the trout population in Long Lake and elsewhere, but they still fight like hell and made a good (when carefully boned) meal. I'm glad Mr. Engels gave them some space in this book.

Let me now confess that when I first saw the title *Adirondack Fishing in the 1930s,* my immediate reaction was, "So what!?" For to me and, I imagine, many others in their mid-sixties, the 1930s seem only yesterday. If Mr. Engels, I thought, had been writting about days when Teddy Roosevelt, or Grover Cleveland, or Winslow Homer were tramping those mountain trails, that would have been something! Then I re-read a report I had just received from the Department of Natural Resources in Ithaca, New York, and I realized with a sense of shock that Mr. Engels' 1930s indeed belonged to an ancient past.

> *ITEM*   Acidification of Adirondack lakes and streams by acid precipitation has resulted in a loss of fish population from many headwater areas. In addition, brief but widespread episodes of high acidity in streams receiving acid snowmelt during late winter and spring thaws result in periods of water quality lethal to fish.

> *ITEM*   . . . Strong inorganic acids (primarily sulfuric and nitric) have dominated the chemis-

150

try of contemporary precipitation . . . since at least the early 1950s. During the past two decades there has been both a regional extension of acid precipitation and an intensification of acidity in the northeast.

ITEM A comprehensive water chemistry and fish survey of 214 high elevation Adirondack lakes reveals that more than half (52 percent) were acidified to levels known to be critical to fish survival, and 82 percent of these acid lakes were found to be devoid of fish life. Comparison with data from the same lakes in the 1930s indicated that formerly viable fish populations had disappeared.

ITEM The increased acidity precipitation has been related to . . . emissions from the combustion of fossil fuels in industrialized regions of the midwest and northeast. These gaseous emissions are transformed into acid aerosols which can be transported long distances before being washed out as acid precipitation. . . . Effects have been particularly severe in the Adirondack region because of the generally low acid-neutralizing capacity of waters draining weather-resistant rock formations composed of granites or gneisses.

Let me add a few observations of my own. One of my favorite Adirondack streams is the South Branch of the Moose River. My friends come back from it boasting of taking some fine "native" brook trout; but they are either lying or ignorant, for a trout stocked in the sections of the Moose I know before the final snow-melt will survive a few days—at best, three. There are practically no holdovers from the previous season in these areas, and all one has to do when the trout has been gutted is to look at the pale, soft white meat which contrasts so vividly with the firm, salmon-pink flesh of the native trout that Mr. Engels knew. A trout caught where I fish the Moose River in July was put there in June, nourished in a commercial hatchery on vitamin-fortified pellets instead of the larvae and insects that give the native trout its unique coloring. As for the lake fish, if the snow-melt has come off a mountain underlain with zinc or aluminum (the aluminum problem is a very recent development) dissolved by the acid fall-out, they have additional toxicity to cope with. Only those lakes shadowed by mountains with limestone deposits (and they are few, will support and nourish the hard-fighting, pink-fleshed native. The Ithaca report offers two solutions: "buffering" the lakes with lime scattered by plane or piled on to rafts strategically placed, or the development of new strains of acid-zinc-aluminum–resistant trout. The first is expensive and is effective for one or two seasons only. The second involves prolonged experimentation and is a long-range proposition.

There is also the "people" factor, and no one has yet come up with a people-resistant trout. Departing the Utica area on a weekend, and driving up Route 12 to the Alder Creek intersection where one turns northeast along Route 28 into the Central Adirondacks, one passes, or, more frequently, is passed by, hundreds of cars trailing inboard and outboard motor boats which might well be, judging from their size and horsepower, destined for the ocean or the St. Lawrence. But no! They will be eased on to mountain lakes, some of which are barely large enough to get up speed and turn around in, towing water skiers, producing washes rugged enough to swamp a canoe or guideboat, and churning up an oily froth along shores lined with empty beer cans and non-biodegradable plastic containers. I won't deny these thrill-seekers their fun, but why not allow, as on some lakes I know in New York State, a time for them (say, between 11 A.M. and 4 P.M.) and a time for the fishermen dawdling along for a wary trout or pike or bass or two? When the snow comes (and it comes early and stays late in the Adirondacks) the trailers will be loaded with snowmobiles which often veer off the trails carefully laid out for them by the Adirondack Park Authority, carving out new trails, cutting down fresh forest growth, and providing runnels for the acid snow-melt.

Each fall, shortly after Labor Day, the lakes of the Fulton Chain—once famed for their "lakers," brook trout, and small-mouth bass—have their water levels lowered as a flood-control measure and at the behest of the owners of long docks built to accommodate gasoline pumps and power boats, and become susceptible to damage. This leaves the shoals and shallows where fish spawn in the fall high and dry, effectively killing off the next season's supply of "natives." Yes, there will be plenty of stunted perch, sunnies, and bullheads left for the kids to catch, for they thrive (and overpopulate) in such "civilized" environments. But the trout fisherman will have to do some strenuous backpacking, or take his chances in a pontoon plane run by a manic bush-pilot who doesn't mind picking up a few pine boughs while landing or taking off on some isolated pond which may or may not have been "acidified."

There are still some fortunate few in the Adirondacks who belong to expensive private clubs where the lakes, if they are small enough, are buffered regularly; where motor boats and water skiing are forbidden, along with winter snowmobiling. Eager young graduate students from Cornell appear each summer. They net, tag, and release the brookies and the rainbows for purposes of growth study. They experiment with dwarf suckers and smelt as food-fish. They spread deadly rotenone across the lakes which have been taken over by sunnies and bullheads whose fertile spawn has been carried in from the public lakes on the legs of wading birds, restocking the lakes with trout after they have lain fallow for a year or two. They post the rivers with signs reading "Fly-fishing Only" and the lakes with "Artificials (single hook) Only." But such enclaves, naturally, are a challenge to outsiders who, quite justifiably, perhaps, in our democratic society, resent these privileged ones with their antique guideboats, their elaborately furnished "camps," and their skilled fish-management crews. Even here, however, one finds tragedy—a loon strangled in a coil of monofilament tossed overboard by a careless spin-caster, streams too swift, and lakes too large for liming and afflicted with "transparency" (when a white disc is lowered to twenty feet or so, and you can still see it, the water, bereft of algae, is far less productive, suitable only for swimming or sailing, or as a passage to some trail leading to a "far lake" that has somehow survived the acid fallout from Detroit, Chicago, Gary, Cleveland, and points west).

What are the answers? For one thing, books like this by Vincent Engels may help—but only if younger Adirondacks lovers than I will read them with a searing sense of the disaster that is overtaking these lovely lakes and streams of ours. As I said earlier I read this book with pleasure and sorrow, but also with anger at the despoilers— especially those greedy ones who want the Adirondack Park Authority (our only guarantee that at least a portion of that land can remain "forever wild") emasculated, so that more lakes, rivers, and mountains can be turned over to the uncaring.

And what about the trout themselves? Well, no fisherman can afford to be anthropomorphic about the fish he kills, though I have a nine-year-old granddaughter who, whenever I give a trout the *coup de grâce,* cries out (not too passionately), "Granddaddy, how gross!" But as Bergman wrote, "the elements of all life, whether human or otherwise, are directly related." When I think of those Adirondack fish struggling to survive in poisoned waters, or trying in vain to perpetuate their species by spawning along shoals that at the crucial time will be left high and dry, I remember a poem by Rupert Brooke called "Heaven"—a fish-eye view of the afterlife:

> Oh, never fly conceals a hook
> Fish say, in that Eternal Brook,
> But more than mundane weeds are there,
> And mud celestially fair;
> Fat caterpillars drift around
> And paridisal grubs are found;
> Unfading moths, immortal flies,
> And the worm that never dies.
> And in that Heaven of all their wish
> There shall be no more land, say fish.

Mr. Engels and I would not, of course, go along with that hookless fly, or a landless Heaven, but I'm sure we both wish our native fish better luck in their "Great Beyond," with no more acid rains or thoughtless two-legged fellow creatures laying waste to the waters they claim to love!

Charles L. Todd

Hamilton, New York

155